West Country Vol II

Edited by Heather Killingray

Young**Writers**
First published in Great Britain in 2004 by:
Young Writers
Remus House
Coltsfoot Drive
Peterborough
PE2 9JX
Telephone: 01733 890066
Website: www.youngwriters.co.uk

SB ISBN 1 84460 494 2

Foreword

Young Writers was established in 1991 and has been passionately devoted to the promotion of reading and writing in children and young adults ever since. The quest continues today. Young Writers remains as committed to engendering the fostering of burgeoning poetic and literary talent as ever.

This year's Young Writers competition has proven as vibrant and dynamic as ever and we are delighted to present a showcase of the best poetry from across the UK. Each poem has been carefully selected from a wealth of *Once Upon A Rhyme* entries before ultimately being published in this, our twelfth primary school poetry series.

Once again, we have been supremely impressed by the overall high quality of the entries we have received. The imagination, energy and creativity which has gone into each young writer's entry made choosing the best poems a challenging and often difficult but ultimately hugely rewarding task - the general high standard of the work submitted amply vindicating this opportunity to bring their poetry to a larger appreciative audience.

We sincerely hope you are pleased with our final selection and that you will enjoy *Once Upon A Rhyme West Country Vol II* for many years to come.

Contents

St Nicholas' Chantry CE School, Clevedon

Sedgemoor Manor Community Junior School, Somerset

The Poems

At The Fair

Twisting, turning, spinning and moving!
Yes it's the rides at the fair.
They're all lit up,
As bright as the sun.
Dodgems here I come!
The music as loud as loud as can be,
Keeping to the beat.
The ghost train alone,
Would chill my feet!
I don't want to go home!

Rhys Baker (9)
Burrowbridge Primary School, Somerset

When I Was One

When I was one I bit my thumb,
When I was two I could see you,
When I was three I climbed a tree,
When I was four I fell on the floor,
When I was five I was still alive,
When I was six I did the splits,
When I was seven I went to Devon,
When I was eight I was great,
When I was nine I walked a line,
When I was ten I built a den,
But I guess it doesn't matter how old I am
Special!

Gemma Ellis (9)
Burrowbridge Primary School, Somerset

Shipwreck

A cold, windy night on the sea,
When something bad happened.
The deep, deafening water grew higher and higher,
Suddenly the waves came crashing against a ship.
Water came running into the door,
It was locked!
There was no escape.
People screamed, shouted and cried.
Somebody *help!*
The water grew higher and higher,
It reached the top of the ship.
The ship went down,
Never to be seen again.

Sophie Fraser (8)
Burrowbridge Primary School, Somerset

My Imaginary Friend

She maybe half see through
But that doesn't bother me
She maybe non-existent
But we're as happy as can be
She's always, always there
No matter where I go
She is not very clever
Because she only knows what I know
Together we do everything
That's how it'll always be
I'll play all day with my special
Friend, just her and me.

Phoebe Stone (9)
Burrowbridge Primary School, Somerset

Magic

Magic is like a colour in a rainbow.
Magic is like tricks with a flag.
Magic is like people in a street.
Magic is like spiders crawling round your feet.
Magic is magic.

Nathan Peppard (9)
Burrowbridge Primary School, Somerset

Ghosts and Ghoulies

In the night when the moon is bright,
the ghosts and ghoulies come out to fight.
They play until the start of day,
oh sun so bright, oh sun so bright.

They roll on the floor and throttle each other,
they scream and shout trying to kill one another.
But never before have they seen a child
so mild as you or me.

Then one bright summer morning
a small ghoulie child came out of its lair.
It said with a yawn, 'I'm not,
I'm not afraid of a puny human kid.'
He was wrong, he was seen, he was . . .
Dead.

Amelia Saunders (8)
Burrowbridge Primary School, Somerset

Glitter

In the middle of the night
When you are in your bed
All the fairies in the wood
Come to play about
With their long, gold, flowing hair
They run and play and shout
Their dresses gleam and glitter
As they dance in the moonlight.

The moon is high above them
In the deep blue sky
The owls fly as they see the moon
They know it's time to go.
Off they flew
As the sun peeped through
The fairies were gone
Soon as the sun shone!

Martha Stone (7)
Burrowbridge Primary School, Somerset

Yu-Gi-Oh 2

A slash of a sword like silver stars,
disappeared like a bolt of lightning.
That light is so bright
I can't even see my beast,
that lightning was like an arrow being shot,
that explosion destroyed my beast.

Freddie Saunders (8)
Burrowbridge Primary School, Somerset

Teachers

Teachers creep around,
will they get found,
they hide in the den,
with their pens,
they write a note,
that they want a coat,
they need a drink,
and they hide in the sink.

They want chocolate muffins,
with their tea,
will they get caught by me,
I hide in the tree,
will they see me,
I see them in their den,
Ben is creeping up on them,
here comes one, comes with a bun.

Kirsty Fraser (10)
Burrowbridge Primary School, Somerset

Penguin Poem

Haddock, cod, squid and plaice
All of them I have to chase
After that I stuff my face

I live at the North Pole
It's at the top of the world
It can get very cold

I love to slide on the ice
Don't go too fast . . .
Ouch! Good advice!

Archie Wolfman (9)
Burrowbridge Primary School, Somerset

Killing Goblin

In an old cave far far away
an angry old goblin stood
guarding Harry Potter's ancient wand.
For the first time the goblin went out to the village
and captured a beautiful princess.
The king and queen ordered a search party
to find their daughter.
The king and queen ordered for a prince
to rescue their daughter
and to kill the goblin.
So the prince set off to the goblin's cave
and found the goblin.
They had a fight but the prince got knocked
against the wall and the stalactite,
came down and killed the goblin.
He looked in the cave and he found two things:
the princess and the wand.
From now on the prince guards the wand.

Oliver McGeown (8)
Burrowbridge Primary School, Somerset

There Once Was A Chimp

There once was a chimp
Called Barnebe Boo
He was one
Well nearly two
One day he got lost
But nobody knew
He was found one day
While looking around the zoo.

Stacey Jade Davies (10)
Combe St Nicholas CEVA Primary School, Somerset

There Once Was A Donkey!

There once was a donkey
Called Chipperty Chip
He had a long nose
And an enormous lip
He lived in Chard
With a rat called Ted
And when he got home
Was sleeping in his bed.

Jordan Annette Williams (10)
Combe St Nicholas CEVA Primary School, Somerset

There Once Was A Cat

There once was a cat
Called Tangly Tay
Who stole some fish
And said he would pay.

Then he disappeared
Without a trace
And ran away
To outer space.

Louise Palmer (9)
Combe St Nicholas CEVA Primary School, Somerset

Beady Eyes Bill

There once was a dog
Called Beady Eyes Bill
He stared at the cat
And said he was ill
The cat said, 'I'll help
To make you feel better.'
So she got out her needles
And made him a sweater.

Rebecca Ross (10)
Combe St Nicholas CEVA Primary School, Somerset

A Monkey Brought A Bat

A monkey brought a bat
But the bat was a brat,
The monkey was angry,
So the bat got ready for combat.

The monkey and the bat were at war,
Until there was a knock at the door.
The monkey answered the door
And there was a claw.

Joshua Martin Chadwick (10)
Combe St Nicholas CEVA Primary School, Somerset

Dilly McDoo

There once was a man
Called Dilly McDoo
He stepped in a puddle
And fell right through
He fell on a spike
That silly McDoo
He walked home
Feeling shaken right through.

Jack Lawrence (10)
Combe St Nicholas CEVA Primary School, Somerset

A Monkey Ate A Cork

There once was a monkey
Called Freddy McNork
He found a bottle
And ate the cork
He went pop
Flew into the air
And landed with a splat
To his total despair.

Joseph Cleal (11)
Combe St Nicholas CEVA Primary School, Somerset

A Monkey Bought Some Water Skis

A monkey bought some water skis
But didn't have a boat.

He asked if he could hire one
But it didn't stay afloat.

He shouted for some help
Because he could not swim.

But since he got rescued
He has been quite grim.

Catherine Atkins (10)
Combe St Nicholas CEVA Primary School, Somerset

Animal Madness

There once was a monkey
Called Silly Billy
He kicked a bee
On to Free Willy
The whale it tossed him
Into the sea
He hit a bomb
He went *Kaboom Kablee!*

Joshua Addison (10)
Combe St Nicholas CEVA Primary School, Somerset

There Once Was A Pig

There once was a piggy,
Called Jimmy McFig,
He liked eating apples,
And always wore a wig.
He went out shopping,
His wig blew away,
So he bought another
The very next day.

Amber Vearncombe (10)
Combe St Nicholas CEVA Primary School, Somerset

The King Found A Dress

There once was a king
Who found a purple dress

He looked at it puzzled
Then thought, *this'll impress.*

He wore it to the ball
Everybody stared.

'What? I look good.'
The king declared.

Lauren Nadine Evans (10)
Combe St Nicholas CEVA Primary School, Somerset

Over The Hills and Far Away

Over the hills
And far away
If you look closely
You can see fairies play
They play games
And jump up and down
At the end of the day
The queen puts on her crown.

Jessica Jade Hayter (9)
Combe St Nicholas CEVA Primary School, Somerset

There Once Was A Tiger

There once was a tiger,
Called Tiggrous Tim.
There was a raft contest,
And Tim landed in the bin.
He tried the next year,
And won with glee.
His partner was the boxer,
Jimmy the Flea.

Olivia Bailey (9)
Combe St Nicholas CEVA Primary School, Somerset

The Ape And The Boat

An ape saw a boat,
On a Saturday night.
But when he got in it,
He got a big fright.

The boat when down,
To the bottom of the sea,
And he lived down there
Till he was 93.

Dean Andrew Wilkins (10)
Combe St Nicholas CEVA Primary School, Somerset

Celtic Blues

The wind on the heather so wild and free
Those miserable Romans won't beat me
I'm up on the hillside all alone
But I don't want to fight, I want to go home.

I want to fight for my country's sake
I don't want to lie down and never wake
The rain falls down on my cheek like tears
Soon I will be confronted with my deepest fears

I want to be with my wife and child
Not here on the battlefield with the wind so wild
There are spears flying as I look around
At all my friends that have fallen to the ground

Our dear Queen Boudicca now is dead
Why couldn't those Romans die instead
The battle is over it's been done
Those rotten Romans sadly had won.

Stacey Cleal (10)
Combe St Nicholas CEVA Primary School, Somerset

Celtic Blues

The wind on the heather is wild and free,
Those miserable Romans won't beat me!

I want to give up I need to come home,
But if I leave, my friends will fight on alone.

I want to be gone, fly away like a bird,
Or somewhere with safety, like a cow in its herd.

My friends are all gone, I stand all alone,
I've dropped to the ground, I've died and they've won.

Grace Eveleigh (11)
Combe St Nicholas CEVA Primary School, Somerset

Celtic War Blues

The wind on the heather is wild and free,
Those miserable Romans won't beat me.

I fight for Boudicca, the queen of us Celts,
If we lose our weapons we'll use our belts.

I'm afraid of nothing, not even to die,
If I stand in one place, this is where I will lie.

Queen Boudicca's dead, we're in disgrace,
And here I stand the wind in my face.

Cory Christopher Stuckey (11)
Combe St Nicholas CEVA Primary School, Somerset

Spooky!

A creak upon the landing,
A knock upon the door,
A scream in the laundry room,
A head upon the floor!

A laugh so clear and spooky,
The knocking of knees,
The crunching of popcorn,
Me in front of the TV!

Rebecca Brown (11)
Compton Dundon CE Primary School, Somerset

A Potion

Round and round the cauldron I go,
All the things that I throw,
A rotten leaf off a tree,
And a bit of water from the sea.

Chop and stir, stir and chop,
Thrown things in with a plop.

In everything goes,
Even dirt from between people's toes,
A feather off a bird's wing,
And a nice shiny thing.

Chop and stir, stir and chop,
Thrown things in with a plop.

Alexandra Bearman (9)
Compton Dundon CE Primary School, Somerset

The Day The Zoo Escaped

The day the zoo escaped
The rabbit hopped out quickly
The slug slid out slowly
The tiger zoomed out proudly
The monkey swung our cheerfully
The mice skipped out lightly
But the sloth sleepily just hung around.

Aimee Jenkins (8)
Compton Dundon CE Primary School, Somerset

Horror In The Chamber

Round about the chamber go
In the chamber people throw
Rotten dinner.
Who's the winner?
Stir and chop, stir and chop.
Add it to the boiling pot.
In the chamber croaks a crow.
What's that noise? I don't know.
For a charm of powerful trouble
Like a hell broth boil and bubble.
Stir and chop, stir and chop
Add that to the boiling pot.

Jordan Lock (9)
Compton Dundon CE Primary School, Somerset

A Yummy Feast

Round about the saucepan throw
In with the chocolate go, go, go
Put in the sweeties and stir it too
Mix it all up till it sticks like glue
Put on the temperature till it's hot, hot, hot
Boil thou first in the charmed pot

Mix and bubble mix and bubble
But watch out for your mum you might get in trouble

Don't want no ancient steak
In the cauldron boil and bake
There should be enough for you and me
But be careful you might burn your tongue too
Ugh! I hate custard with lots of lumps
But I love chocolate smooth no bumps
For a charm of powerful trouble
Like a hell broth boil and bubble

Mix and bubble mix and bubble
But watch out for your mum you might get in trouble

Once upon a story
There was a witch who sat in glory
For all the world to see
She cooked for everyone and me
She made a dish so lovely it took us by surprise
It made us forgive all her sins and lies.

Rose Thurston (10)
Compton Dundon CE Primary School, Somerset

Spell

Round about the chamber pot go
In the manky cabbage throw
The vile acid makes it bubble
Do not smell! It makes you see double.

Hubble bubble toil and trouble
Toadstool mix makes powder for tricks
Sole of shoe, oil of car
Beats the smell of droppings by far.

Hubble bubble toil and trouble
Toadstool mix makes power for tricks.

Rowan McMahon (9)
Compton Dundon CE Primary School, Somerset

My Poem

I am scared of the dark,
Like paper is afraid of scissors,
Like corn is afraid of a combine,
Like a bird or falling to the ground,

Like a fish is afraid of a hook,
Like a star is afraid of the sun,
Like an elephant is afraid of a mouse,
Like rubbish is afraid of fire,

Like a cat is afraid of the water,
Like a piece of wood is afraid of a chainsaw,
Like a car is afraid of water,
I'm scared of the dark.

Charlie Merriman (10)
Compton Dundon CE Primary School, Somerset

The Day The Zoo Escaped

The day the zoo escaped,
The monkeys skipped out strangely,
The pony galloped out laughing,

The zebras zigzagged out neatly,
The rabbits hopped out happily,

The spiders crawled out scarily,
The turtle stumbled out slowly,
But
the
sloth
just
sleepily
hung
around.

Vicky Merriman (9)
Compton Dundon CE Primary School, Somerset

The White Falcon

The white falcon,
A British bird of prey,
Fiery, majestic, fast.
Like a flying dart,
Like a ninja stalking his opponent.
It makes me feel small and slow.
The white falcon,
Dives to the ground at record speed.

Nicholas Jones (8)
East Huntspill Primary School, Somerset

The Magnificent . . .

The magnificent horse.
My horse is black like the rain clouds on a stormy day.
His flowing mane is like the tassels on a rug.
His shiny tail shines like black silk.
His strong hooves are like big, gold shoes.
He resembles an exploding black rocket racing in the field.
I will not let him be taken away from me.
I will ride him bareback every day and care for him.

Kiira Gilvear (7)
East Huntspill Primary School, Somerset

The Magnificent . . .

The magnificent shark.
My shark is strong like one hundred strong men lifting boulders.
His rubbery skin is like a slithery snake sliding through grease,
His black eyes are like pieces of coal.
His teeth are like sharp blades on a flick-knife.
He resembles an Olympic swimmer.
I will protect him.

Sophie Brewer (8)
East Huntspill Primary School, Somerset

The Magnificent . . .

The magnificent cat.
My cat is fluffy like cotton wool.
His claws are like sharp needles.
His long tail is like a piece of string.
His glowing eyes are like fire in the night.
He resembles a multi-coloured coat.
I will love him all my life and I will feed him.

Lisa Butt (7)
East Huntspill Primary School, Somerset

The Magnificent . . .

The magnificent crocodile
My crocodile is motionless like a log in a swamp.
His bumpy skin is like the rough bark on a tree,
His evil looking eyes are like two glowing red-hot embers.
His sharp pointed teeth are like sabres.
He resembles a snappy, murderous killer.
I will protect him and give him the space to live.

Jordan Lockyer (9)
East Huntspill Primary School, Somerset

The Magnificent . . .

The magnificent dog.
My dog is black like smoke curling from a chimney.
His fur is like a teddy bear.
His tail is like a long piece of string.
His claws are like sharp forks.
He resembles a soft and well-loved teddy bear.
I will love him and feed him.

Daisi-Anna Pugsley (8)
East Huntspill Primary School, Somerset

Jack And The Beanstalk

She snatched the beans, she yelled, 'You chump!'
She swallowed them whole with a bump,
Then summoning up all her power,
She grabbed the boy and locked him in the tower
(and nothing could be meaner),
Her friend called round, her name was Tina
At 10pm or there about.
The little bean was growing quick, quick, quick.
By morning it had grown so tall
You couldn't see his mum at all.

David Horton (10)
Manor Court Community Primary School, Somerset

Round The Clock

I'm sleeping round the clock,
Dreams turning like a lock.
I don't think I'll ever wake up,
How must I look?

I'm such a great big sleepy head,
Always in my bed.
I don't think I'll ever buy any leather.

I'm always sleeping,
It's enough to make you start weeping,
I'm always so tired,
I think I'll be fired!

I'm sleeping round the clock,
I think you're going to mock!

Thomas Wicklen (10)
Manor Court Community Primary School, Somerset

Two Little Guinea Pigs

Two little guinea pigs went for a run
Later it became sunny and they had some fun
They played all day and they slept all night
Until the next day was sunny and bright
Then it was the end of the day
They slept all night hoping that the next day they could play
Hoping that it would be sunny just like yesterday
The next morning they woke up with a fright
They found out that the next morning wasn't sunny and bright
They squeaked and squeaked but the sun never came
So they sat in their hutch, ate a carrot and played a game.

Megan Trott (10)
Manor Court Community Primary School, Somerset

Ladybirds!

Ladybirds, ladybirds, creep me out,
Crawling along the walls,
Ladybirds, ladybirds creep me out,
The spots on their backs, like big black balls.
Ladybirds, ladybirds creep me out,
Fly away, fly away, leave me alone,
Ladybirds, ladybirds creep me out,
I shout, I scream, I moan,
Ladybirds, ladybirds creep me out,
Especially in the summer,
Ladybirds, ladybirds creep me out,
Oh why do I bother?

Hollie Keri Broome (10)
Manor Court Community Primary School, Somerset

The Spiders

Spiders creep me out
When I go in my room.
The moon comes out
All I do is look at it,
It really has got 8 legs,
It is really disgusting,
I can't go to sleep.
My sister is in a stress
I hate being woken when I'm asleep
When I woke up, the spider was still there
When I got back from school it was gone.

Cody Hall (11)
Manor Court Community Primary School, Somerset

The Odd Teacher

They say he's mean
They say he growls
They say he punishes
They say he's proud
They say he's weird
They say he's cool
They say he's obnoxious
And they say he's loud.

He can be mean
He does growl
He does punish
He is proud
He is weird
He is cool
He is obnoxious
And he's definitely . . .
Loud!

Hannah Hall (11)
Manor Court Community Primary School, Somerset

Head Collecting Sounds

Mr Flowers called this morning,
Dressed in suit and tie,
To check how noisy children were,
And then he started to cry.

The whistling of the wind,
The turning of the tyres,
The thudding of the footsteps,
The buzzing of the wires.

James Hall-Roberts (10)
Manor Court Community Primary School, Somerset

The Creep Of The Deep

The creep of the deep
Comes out for a peep
Once in a full blue moon
His partner a really big goon
I reckon they'll get me soon.

A spine of spikes
Scared eyes he likes
His claws and paws
With his teeth he gnaws
Oh no he's knocking down doors
Run, run, run for the moors.

The creep of the deep
Comes for a peep
Once in a full blue moon.

Sam Bennett (11)
Manor Court Community Primary School, Somerset

Monkey!

Tree jumper
twig climber
banana eater
furry creature
food taker
tree shelterer
quick mover
noise maker
swish swash tail
likes to yell.
Oh ah ah the noise it makes
while it's walking by the lake.

Katy Greenway (10)
Manor Court Community Primary School, Somerset

What Is It?

Water squirter
Hard hurter

Banana eater
Mild sleeper

Colour grey
Never play

Water drinker
Big stinker

Answer: *elephant.*

Kirsty Parsons (10)
Manor Court Community Primary School, Somerset

Snow White

Snow White fell fast asleep
That is when the dwarfs did weep
She was to awaken to a true love's kiss
All the princess the dwarfs did miss

Then one day came along
A handsome prince who had done no wrong
He heard about poor Snow White
And he just knew it wasn't right.

So he jumped on his steed
And fought through the weeds
He then came to a tower
And picked such a beautiful flower

Then Snow White was lying there
And the prince stopped to stare
So he gave her a true love's kiss
No longer Snow White will be missed.

Rebecca Stead (11)
Manor Court Community Primary School, Somerset

Jack Frost

The streets are full of white cold ice,
And snow is falling - it's rather nice,
But the bitter cold drives everyone away,
They are all angry and they say,
It's all because of - Jack Frost.

Everyone's got to wrap up warm,
And keep inside - away from it all,
The children scream and stamp about,
They're angry cos they can't, they can't go out,
It's all because of - Jack Frost.

He walks around with an evil stare,
That freezes everyone - everywhere,
And patterns appear on the door,
People's hands begin to get sore,
Just because of - Jack Frost.

The boilers break cos it's so cold,
The hot chocolate has been sold,
And everyone is inside,
The sun has seemed to have died,
All because of - Jack Frost.

He pierces the heart and makes it hard,
And everyone around Chard,
Stays in and loses all their friends,
They're starved of happiness and send
Blackmail to that evil man - *Jack Frost!*

Emma Aston (11)
Manor Court Community Primary School, Somerset

The Sound Collector

Mr Flowers called this morning
Dressed in suit and tie
To check how noisy the children were
And then he started to cry.

The whistling of the wind,
The turning of the handle,
The squeaking of the car wheel,
The ticking of the clock.

The popping of the pens,
The crunching of the paper,
The shouting of the children,
The hissing of the cat.

Mr Flowers called this morning,
Still crying.

Nathan Quick (10)
Manor Court Community Primary School, Somerset

Rhyme Time

I like rhyming words I've liked them all my life.

The ticking of the clock
The turning of the lock
The pitter patter of the rain
The water going down the drain.

The growling of a dog
The rolling rumble of a log
The bubbling of the kettle
The breathing of the baby as it starts to settle.

The tapping of your feet
The crunching as you eat
Some of them are dull and grey
But I like to carry them anyway.

Georgina Stevens (10)
Manor Court Community Primary School, Somerset

Dog

Quad legger
Big beggar

Fast runner
Like a gunner

Wet nose
4 toes

Fur licker
Rabbit kicker

Long sleeper
Bone eater

Open locks
Shredded up box

Bright eyed
Takes corners wide

Likes to walk
It will talk

Dog.

Tom Holloway (11)
Manor Court Community Primary School, Somerset

What Is It?

An angry boar
Who lives on the shore
He snaps and bites
And wears red tights
He walks sideways
All of the days
He's very yummy
In my tummy
What is it?
Of course it's a . . .
Crab!

Matt Cridge (11)
Manor Court Community Primary School, Somerset

Huish Park

The whistle has blown.
The fans start to groan,
Yeovil start winning,
The fans are singing,
The keeper made a save,
He rescued the day,
What's he going to do?

Kevin Gall scores,
The crowd adores,
Him, him only,
A manager was lonely,
Kevin done it solo,
He wanted a polo,
What's he going to do?

Jamie Harris (10)
Manor Court Community Primary School, Somerset

The Monster Under The Stairs

The monster is under the stairs
His favourite food is pears
He lives in a pile of grit
He is a bit of a twit
The monster is under the stairs
He really likes bears
He supports Aston Villa
He wishes they could sign Miller
He watches the telly
While he fills up his belly
When 12 o'clock hits
He gets out his pit
And gets out from under the stairs
He goes into my room
With a broom
And frightens the lights out of me.

Nathan Warren (10)
Manor Court Community Primary School, Somerset

The Red Beast

Red beast
At the very least

When it starts
It don't bark

Turn the ignition
You'll start demolition

Take it to the city
No one can say pity

It's number one
Just for fun

It's there for pleasure
That you just can't measure

So take it on a ride
It's not there to hide.

Ashley Harris (11)
Manor Court Community Primary School, Somerset

The Continued Cinderella Story!

No I am not alright
It's really really late at night
Cinderella jumped up high
With a nasty horrible cry.

'I want to go to the ball,
But I look like a fool!
I really fancy that guy
And he *will* say goodbye.'

He tore my dress, I lost my slipper,
And I found a kipper.

Lauren Dawn Birch (11)
Manor Court Community Primary School, Somerset

The Weird Version of Jack And The Beanstalk

'Jack go out and sell our cow
And run get out there right now
We haven't got any dosh
You you'd better find someone posh.'
'Oh look, oh look, Mumsie dear
I sold her for a pint of beer
And look I got some magic beans
To buy a pear of Levi jeans.'
'Oh you stupid, stupid boy
I'll sell you for a cuddly toy
Now go to bed without any supper
You silly, silly little sucker.'
He saw his mum chuck them out the window
While he was playing on his Nintendo
He woke up in the sunny morning
While he was badly yawning
His mum was really screaming
When he thought he was dreaming
He ran downstairs and out the door
And on my God look at the floor
He climbed up the gigantic stalk
When he found a joint of pork
And sticking out a massive fork
Then a voice said 'Oy, you dork
I'll eat you up like your mum
And beat you like a massive drum'
'I'm going to stab you with this fork
Now who's the big fat dork!'

Josh Hamer (11)
Manor Court Community Primary School, Somerset

My Day

I went for a run
at half past one,
I bought a shoe
at half past two,
I got my key
at half past three,
I opened my door
at half past four,
I went for a drive
at half past five,
I ate a Twix
at half past six,
I felt like I was in Heaven
at half past seven,
I saw my mate
at half past eight,
I had some wine
at half past nine,
I went in my den
at half past ten.

Jacob Hardiman (11)
Manor Court Community Primary School, Somerset

Cinderella - How It Really Happened

No I'm not alright
It's really, really late at night,
Cinderella jumped up high,
With a nasty horrible cry.

I want to go to the ball,
But I look like a fool,
I really fancy that guy,
And he may well say goodbye.

Finally I arrived at the ball,
Meeting the prince he was very tall,
As the clock struck 12:00 I ran down the stairs
And lost my slipper,
As I ran home to feed the sisters their kipper.

'Marry me,' the prince asked I,
Looking at me with his blue eyes,
I walked off with the prince,
Then he looked at me with a glance.

Emma Newbery (10)
Manor Court Community Primary School, Somerset

It Doesn't Make Any Sense

How can I walk on thin air?
It can't get any thinner.

How can I pick up my feet?
I won't be able to walk.

How can I take off my hair?
It's solid, glued to my head.

I don't want to break a leg
Or any bone for that matter.

Laura Bide (10)
Manor Court Community Primary School, Somerset

The Ghost Sound Collector

A ghost of a little boy called this morning,
Dressed in white and grey,
Put all the sounds in his school bag,
And carried them away today.

The whistling of the wind,
The turning of the big loader,
The squeaking of the pens
The ticking of the cooler.

The popping of the pen lids,
The crunching of the leaves,
The shouting of the teacher,
The sizzling of the beef.

A ghost of a little boy called this morning,
And did not leave his name,
And did not give the sounds back,
This was not our aim.

Jake Genge (10)
Manor Court Community Primary School, Somerset

Louis Saha

L ate arrival best in the biz
O pting to Man Utd greatest there could be
U sing dazzling skills scoring on his debut
I nvited to our team, I wish he could
S izzling hot as fast as I have seen

S assy boots no one could buy
A ching legs still works hard
H uffing and puffing work rate is still high
A way game decides the champs guess who scores our Man.

George Fowler (11)
Manor Court Community Primary School, Somerset

Untitled

(My own version of Roald Dahl's 'Revolting Rhymes' continued halfway through)

No, I am not alright,
It's really, really late at night
Cinderella jumped up high,
With a big sad horrendous cry.

'I want to get to the ball,
But I look like such a fool.
I really do fancy that guy,
And he may well say goodbye.'

The fairy godmother came to say,
'Make a wonderful wish today.'
I met the prince at the ball
I didn't realise that he was so tall.

He said he wanted to marry me
So then I said, 'Maybe,'
I ran so fast to the carriage
And then I thought about marriage.

I lost my slipper on the way
I thought he'd come with it someday
In the end I got married
And I thought I would be married.

Carly Board (11)
Manor Court Community Primary School, Somerset

That's Tiffany My Best Friend!

She's mad and crazy
Sometimes very lazy
She thinks she's very funny
She's cuddly like a bunny
That's Tiffany, my best friend!

She drives you up the wall
But be careful you don't fall
She's sometimes very clumsy
And sometimes very mumsie
That's Tiffany, my best friend!

But the thing that she likes most
Is eating a stack of toast
She likes the name Kerrie
But not the name Terry
That's Tiffany, my best friend!

Her room is silver and blue
But has no news for you
Her guinea pig is grey
And always like to play
That's Tiffany, my best friend.

Sophie Louise Gummer (11)
Manor Court Community Primary School, Somerset

Mr Flowers Called This Morning

Mr Flowers called this morning,
Dressed in a suit and tie,
To check how noisy children were,
And then he started to cry.

Miss Howard said to go and get a tissue,
Before his lovely suit got damp,
But when he got to the staff room,
He got a horrible cramp.

Mr Flowers called this morning,
He scared me half to death,
He stayed a moment or two,
Then all of a sudden he left.

Holly Baker (11)
Manor Court Community Primary School, Somerset

Cinderella Story Continued

Yes, I'm ok but can your wand whisk me away?
All I want to do is to go out to play.

I will try my best, put myself to the test,
How did I get myself in such a mess?

I want to go to the ball, but I look like a ghoul,
I really love that guy and he will say goodbye.

He tore my dress and ripped my hair, now I look like Bess.
I will give you 3 wishes and she gave a few hisses.

I want to go to a ball, with my prince in the hall.
I will make you not look like a ghoul and take you to the ball.

I am finally at the ball, the prince is so tall,
So I ran away, lost my slipper and sock on the way.

Zoe Stevenson (10)
Manor Court Community Primary School, Somerset

Mr Flowers Called This Morning

Mr Flowers called this morning,
Dressed in suit and tie,
To check how noisy children were,
And then he started to cry.

The stamping of the children running,
The screams of the bleeding knees,
The teachers saying, 'Don't worry,'
The swishing of the trees.

Mr Flowers called this morning,
And didn't leave a sound,
He wished it could be quiet,
And his heart started to pound.

Kristina Ryan (11)
Manor Court Community Primary School, Somerset

Trucks

Trucks, trucks they are so mucky,
Trucks, trucks they are a pain,
Trucks, trucks they are so mad,
Trucks, trucks they are insane.

Trucks, trucks, they do go fast,
Trucks, trucks they do break down,
Trucks, trucks as they go past,
Trucks, trucks, they make a good sound.

Trucks, trucks they do have feelings,
Trucks, trucks they do smell like diesel,
Trucks, trucks they do get sad,
Trucks, trucks they do go out of fashion.

Matthew Slade (11)
Manor Court Community Primary School, Somerset

Football

Hernan Crespo, what a star
Hits the ball, hit the bar
Duff on to it . . .
Goal! He hit that with his soul
1 - 0 to the blues
What amazing news!
The other team on the attack
The defender turns his back
He's slipped
He goes for a chip
What a save from the keeper
It was always getting deeper
The final whistle goes.

Liam Cleal (11)
Manor Court Community Primary School, Somerset

Me And My Friends

Me and my friends go out to play every single day,
We have a merry day.
We go from place to place
And make a load of noise
On the way up through the town
Me and my friends play loads of games
We go into some fields then get other things to do
On our way home, we have a lot of fun,
Some of us go in our friend's houses
And when we get home, we tell what
We did that day.

Daniel Dearden (11)
Manor Court Community Primary School, Somerset

Dad's DIY Disaster

My dad hates DIY
He always patches stuff up with ply
One day my dad ran out of ply
You could see through the roof, up to the sky
All my mum could do was cry
Even my dog Kyle
She gave a great big sigh
My mum said, 'That's it, there's no more you and I!'

Ashley Day (11)
Manor Court Community Primary School, Somerset

Ming Mong

When the cows go ming
And the boys go mong
The brains go ping
And the girls go pong
When the books go ding
And the bells go dong
The birds go ring
And the teachers go wrong
The rabbits go bing
And the pencils go bong
The mice go ting
And the birds go tong
The dogs go king
And the cats go kong
But the monkeys all shout
'Ming! Mong! Ping! Pong!
Ding! Dong! Bing! Bong!
Ring! Wrong! Ting! Tong!
King! Kong!'

Adam Stevenson (11)
Manor Court Community Primary School, Somerset

The Wind

The wind will blow you away,
The wind will keep you awake at night.

The wind can be stronger than you are,
The wind whistles through the air.

The wind blows hair in the faces of strangers,
The wind is a mini tornado.

The wind will knock trees down,
The wind can make the leaves fall off.

Becky Pullinger (11)
Milton Junior School, Weston-super-Mare

Volcano

The volcano's anger storming through the air,
Its eyes frowning across empty woods.
The roar as it wakes up to clobber the land,
Its cough, as if it was never heard before.
The blood trickling down its worried face.

Joshua Morgan (11)
Milton Junior School, Weston-super-Mare

All About Friends

My friends are sweet.
My friends are kind,
No matter what people do they're always there.
They always play with me,
No matter what they say,
No matter what they do -
If I'm upset they always ask me if I'm okay.
My friends are kind
My friends are sweet.

Ashleigh Sweeney (10)
Milton Junior School, Weston-super-Mare

The Park

The leaves bustle in and out of the people,
Down the hill, jogging to the park.
Through the gates, into the park,
In and out of the trees with long, spindly fingers.
The wind whistles in and out of the trees' long arms.
Listening to the sound of children playing.
Down to the swings, dancing to the wind bustling
The slide, watching with pleasure.
The roundabout spins round in delight, at watching
The clever swings
Then everything goes quiet.
The sun closes its eyes.

Rebecca Durston (11)
Milton Junior School, Weston-super-Mare

The Wind Rustled

The wind rustled in and out of the fingers of the trees
Wakening them in the morning, noon and night.

The eyes of the car flashed on and off
Letting another car move first

The motorbike roared into life
When the lights turned green

The sea digs into the sandy beach
Creeping closer and closer towards the street

The wheel of a bike jogging over the cobbly road
In its own marathon race.

The clock comes to life,
Chuckling when the seconds go by.

Natalie Culliven (11)
Milton Junior School, Weston-super-Mare

Life Town

The buildings sulk, standing still all day
When it rains they sulk more, no shelter to go under.

The cars slither across the road,
With anger of the busy town.

The sun falls, the light posts wake up
To work and smile.

The train crawls along the track
Screaming to stop at a station.

The plane fights through the clouds,
Beating all of them.

The wind gets angry over the town.

Michael Carter (11)
Milton Junior School, Weston-super-Mare

The Ever Moving City

I had a view of the smiling buildings,
Which stared with all of their hundreds of eyes.

As the snake of cars, slithered through a giant maze,
While they coughed and spluttered about.

While the smoke held onto the windows,
As they floated up to the sky.

The rubbish crawled right up the street
While leaving its trail behind.

I walked down the stairs while the lift was swallowed underground
To be pushed up once again.

I got onto the subway to leave the town
As it crawled its way to the next.

Tom Fealey (11)
Milton Junior School, Weston-super-Mare

Morning Time

The morning sun opens its eyes with
Beaming light shining on the village below
Frost creeping down the windows
To let the houses wake up and now

Cars wake up with roaring anger and warm up their insides
They do not appreciate the wait when they take us for rides

Their arms rub the frost from their face
Their feet start spinning for a race

Roaring with pain when it crashes
He's under stress because he didn't brake
All its power, running low
It's had no food for a week or so

It stops to a halt and starts to sleep
It is now silent - not a peep!

Polly Notley (11)
Milton Junior School, Weston-super-Mare

The Wind

The wind whistles while it tries to
Work its way through the rough trees.
The wind will blow you away
If you annoy him.
The wind kicks up the leaves in the air.
The wind is tough and rough
And could take you any day.
In the morning, the wind yawns
Loudly it could suck you in.
Slowly the wind dies and it dies slower and slower.

Katy Limbert (10)
Milton Junior School, Weston-super-Mare

The Wind

When the wind is angry
It hovers up the leaves and spits them out

As the wind flexes its muscles
To blow the leaves off the trees

When it's made enough mess
It curls up in bed
And sleeps.

Josh Horler (11)
Milton Junior School, Weston-super-Mare

The Lonely Unicorn

The unicorn is magnificent, the unicorn is white
The unicorn is sobbing in the moonlight

As the tears trickle down his cheeks
He looked up at the misty peaks

The lonely unicorn lets out a sigh
Wanting a friend until morning is nigh

The unicorn really wants a friend
Until his life came to an end

But he said, 'I hurt a wrist
And nobody thinks I even exist.'

So the unicorn let a yawn
He looked up once more and saw a fawn

'At last!' he said. 'My loneliness is through.
We'll fly over the peaks, just me and you.'

And they flew over the rocky peak
And the unicorn is what you seek

Try and see them at dawn
The lonely unicorn and the little fawn.

Ben Kettleborough (9)
Milton Junior School, Weston-super-Mare

The Grandfather Clock

The clock chimed slowly
As it came to eleven o'clock

Its hands ticked to eleven
It never-ever stopped

The clock sits on the fireplace
All day and all night

Wakes up in the morning,
What a wonderful sight.

Its hands are always moving
He always tells the time.

Even when he's sleeping
Till half-past nine.

Poppy Carson (11)
Milton Junior School, Weston-super-Mare

The Human Wind

The wind runs so fast through
The back alleys
While scooping up tons of
Rubbish on the way

The wind in a temper, is not
A pretty sight
Wind's so fast, anything in
Its way, is destroyed.

The wind is kind and joyful
In a good mood, he whistles
A joyful song
This is the wind and he is alive!

Zachary Burgess (10)
Milton Junior School, Weston-super-Mare

Hurry Up!

Let's get tidying,
Pack away the games.
Rubbish in the bin,
Quickly, quickly James!
Start running,
Teacher's coming,
To your seats.
Stop that humming!

Hurry, hurry!
She's coming through the door,
Quick sit down!
Oh no, there's an apple core!

We're almost tidied,
Come on go!
There's some paper on the floor,
Oh no!

Sharpen your pencil,
We're wasting time.
Hurry up, she's coming!
Hey - don't take that, that's mine!

Hayley Smith (9)
Milton Junior School, Weston-super-Mare

The Wind

The wind kicks up all of the leaves,
And spins like a spiral.
As it tries to fight its way through the thunder.

It whistles as it goes down the street
And the leaves run across the floor, taking
Sticks and twigs with it.
As it passes the trees, they bow as if the wind
Was the queen or king,
But all it is, is the wind.

Danielle Hancock (11)
Milton Junior School, Weston-super-Mare

The Stormy Town

The cars rumble with anger in the busy town,
The grey clouds frown at the helpless people.

The train pulls with its long arms along
The laughing, slippery track.

The rough sea lashes out at surviving boats.
The plane fights through the rumbling, angry night sky,
The towering buildings whimper as the lightning fires itself at it.

Josh Tyler (11)
Milton Junior School, Weston-super-Mare

Clarinet

C is for clarinet players
L is for learning
A is for applause at the end of the song
R is for rehearsing
I is for interesting
N is for never stop blowing
E is for enjoyable
T is for trying your best.

Emily Burt (11)
North Newton Primary School, Somerset

Rabbits

R is for running rabbit
A is for apple eating bunny
B is for bouncing bunny
B is for busy bees when I hold my bunny
I is for *I* have to clean out the hutch
T is for time to feed my rabbit
S is for sleeping bunny curled up in bed.

Emily Forbes-Buckingham (10)
North Newton Primary School, Somerset

Christmas

C hristmas crackers, banging loudly
H appy people, having fun
R ipping paper to find what's inside
I n church, singing to the Holy Spirit
S inging carols in the snow
T ea being spilled on the Christmas tree
M um checking the turkey and getting tired
A ll people playing with their presents
S aws cutting trees, ready for Christmas.

Tom Baker (9)
North Newton Primary School, Somerset

Sailing

S ail over clear waters
A ll over the world
I n storms and peace
L ighthouses show all the sharp rocks
I n and out of the waves
N ice and enjoyable trips
G oing on into the night.

James Hugh (11)
North Newton Primary School, Somerset

Dragons

Dragons, fire-breathing monsters,
A scaly, evil killing machine.
Armies have fought them,
With their spears, bows and swords
But they haven't been enough to slay them.

Scott Cook (9)
North Newton Primary School, Somerset

The Star Cat

S is for shooting magic stars
T is for twinkling moons
A is for apples, falling gracefully
R is for rainbows, magically appearing

C is for cats, singing in space
A is for alley cats, running on Mars
T is for The Star Cat, the best cat of all.

India Stock (9)
North Newton Primary School, Somerset

Christmas

C is for Christmas cards
H is for happiness, all around
R is for ripping open presents
I is for in church, singing carols
S is for singing
T is for twinkling tree
M is for Mum, checking the turkey
A is for all people, playing with their presents
S is for Santa, coming down the chimney.

Francesca Watts (9)
North Newton Primary School, Somerset

Bunnies

B unnies snuggling near their Mum
U nknown things, ready to be discovered.
N ewly opened flowers, all beautiful and bright and full of colour.
N ew lambs skipping in the fields,
I ndigo, a colour of the rainbow in the sky.
E ggs with chicks ready to hatch out, all yellow and fluffy.
S pring is here and is as beautiful as ever.

Jessica Barham (9)
North Newton Primary School, Somerset

Christmas

C is for crackers at the table
H is for happiness
R is for reindeer
I is for ivy
S is for stocking
T is for Christmas trees
M is for Merry Christmas
A is for angel
S is for Santa.

David Carney (9)
North Newton Primary School, Somerset

Monsters

M onsters are evil
O n the way to destroy
N o one's axes could bring them down
S pace monster
T errifying
E normous monster sleep in their lairs
R oaming the sky
S caly slivery monster.

Thomas Outram (10)
North Newton Primary School, Somerset

The Gryphon

This fabulous beast is most noble, to its master.
Half lion, half eagle.
Gracefully swooping down,
Clutching deer in its razor sharp talons,
Then flying away.

Liam Wilkins (9)
North Newton Primary School, Somerset

Christmas Dog

C is for a Christmas dog
H is for happy dogs and people
R is for rats, sniffing round the rubbish
I is for icing on the cake
S is for snow, drifting down
T is for tummies rumbling
M is for Mum's cooking
A is for after dinner mints
S is for snow dogs, pulling sleighs

D is for dogs everywhere
O is for opening cans
G is for getting presents.

Yasmin Fox (10)
North Newton Primary School, Somerset

Birds In My Garden

G is for grass
A is for apple trees
R is for robin
D is for dune
E is for evergreen trees
N is for nests

B is for birds
I is for ice
R is for rain
D is for Dunnock
S is for swallow.

William Hugh (8)
North Newton Primary School, Somerset

The White Horses

Prancing in the sea,
Galloping along the sand,
I see the white horses
Having races.
Jumping over rocks,
I want to touch them.
Walking in the open,
I touch them, they disappear.

Lucy Boyer (9)
North Newton Primary School, Somerset

The Seaside

S is for slippery rocks
E is for the election of the lifeguard
A is for anchors, clanking on the bottom of the ocean
S is salty seawater
I is for creamy ice cream
D is for dogs swimming excitedly
E is for enjoying a swim in the sea.

Benjamin Samuel Williams (8)
North Newton Primary School, Somerset

Cooking

If you are no good at cooking
I will be crying
Because I am hungry to death.

I am going to sue you
But Mum, I haven't cooked
Since I was a kid or in cooking school.
So this is the first time I've cooked
I will cook, fish and chips
And then drink beer and go to bed.
I will sleep, dreaming of food.

Sam Cottey (9)
North Newton Primary School, Somerset

Birds

B irds fly in the air
I n and out, all about
R obins, sparrows and other birds
D ead, black feet
S ilent at night, awake in the morning.

Jack Hellier (9)
North Newton Primary School, Somerset

Armadillos

A is for armadillos curling into balls
R is for rolling up, if they are scared.
M is for made-up shell of brown armour
D is for dirty, most of the time.
I is for irregular feet,
L is for little pointy ears.
L is for long nose
O is for orange sand, sticking to them
S is for short, stubby legs.

Cameron Luke Street (8)
North Newton Primary School, Somerset

Christmas

C is for crackers
H is for happy
R is for Rudolph
I is for ivy
S is for Santa
T is for Christmas tree
M is for mistletoe
A is for angel
S is for snowballs.

Callum Forbes-Buckingham (8)
North Newton Primary School, Somerset

Transport

Tractors and trains
Diggers and cranes
Buses and planes
All on the move

Big and small vans
Coach loads of fans
Smart caravans
All on the move

Big juggernauts
Ferries in ports
Bikes for all sports
All on the move.

Dominic Turner (10)
Oake & Bradford CP School, Taunton

Hungry For Pie

When I am hungry
I love to eat pie
Oh my, oh my
I love to eat pie
Be it apple or cherry or plum
I love it, yum, yum!
Whether it's cold or hot
Even warm pie hits the spot
I love it with cream or custard
Though I could never eat it with mustard
But of all the pies in all the land
My favourite has to be
A big meat pie
Covered in gravy!

Josh Burgess (10)
Oake & Bradford CP School, Taunton

The Unicorn

She's very big and very strong
She sings a lot of weather
Songs.

She's clear and white
With so much might.

A horn so bright,
A shine of light.
And a mystery too hard
For a snake!

Verryan Kelly (9)
Oake & Bradford CP School, Taunton

Space

Space, space,
Is a very open place.
There are planets, all making a face.

Stars are scattered
Around the sun.
To go into space, would be good fun.

Michael Benn (10)
Oake & Bradford CP School, Taunton

The Shark

T he shark has rough, wrinkly and tough skin
H is enemy is the dolphin
E ventually some sharks can grow up to 280 teeth.

S harks have big clutching jaws
H e eats fish or plankton and sometimes even seals
A nd there are lots of different species of sharks
R azor-sharp teeth, they have
K illing is their job.

George Loader (11)
Oake & Bradford CP School, Taunton

Alone In A Field

Alone in a field, beneath a tree
With no one for company, not even a bee.
Beads of rain running down his flank,
Look into his eyes, gaunt and sank.
Shabby black coat stretched over his frame
Never loved, never given a name.

A tight head collar, cutting into his face
He could have been great, maybe won a race.
His owner had left him here to perish
He needed someone whom he could cherish.

The beaten horse looked up at the sky
Blinking a horsey tear from his eye
A sudden noise came to his ears
A cry of joy, even cheers!

A girl ran towards him, her arms outstretched
She flung her arms around his neck.
She removed the head collar and held his mane,
'Come on old chap, it's tipping with rain!'

So out of the field is the way they went,
With the battered old horse, weak and spent.
Into the horse box he was loaded
With his new owner, keen and devoted.
As he was settled into his warm, new stall
Maybe it would be a happy ending, after all!

Georgina Rose (11)
Oake & Bradford CP School, Taunton

Dogs

In my house I have a dog called Babe,
Who lies in her bed.
At the park, she chases squirrels and birds,
When we get home, she has her tea and
Then she plays with me.
She likes making friends,
So come along and see her.

Jordan Puckett (9)
Oake & Bradford CP School, Taunton

The Red Rose

In the morning sunlight
In the warm breeze
Standing tall
The most beautiful flower of them all
Shining in the sunlight
It is the red rose.

When people walk past, they all say . . .
'This is the most beautiful flower I have seen today.'
They stay there for hours and hours,
They don't like any other flowers.

In the morning sunlight
In the warm breeze
Standing tall
The most beautiful flower of them all
Shining in the sunlight
It is the red rose.

One day a wild wind came along
And the red rose flew away
And from that day on, it was
Never seen again.

Bethany Slack (10)
Oake & Bradford CP School, Taunton

The Gihouse Who Tried To Eat My Shoes

I once knew a gihouse who tried to eat my shoes,
He was yellow with a roof upon his back,
He lived in the field down the river.
Every day, he would come to my house
And try to eat my shoes!
Then one day I happened to notice he had gone,
Maybe he has gone to eat your shoes!
You never know!

Sophie Davies (11)
Oake & Bradford CP School, Taunton

Family

Things were tough
For a while
But I look back
And I can smile
My family's only made of three
But I know that they love me.

Tyronne Patrick (10)
Oake & Bradford CP School, Taunton

My Teacher

My teacher is a chocoholic
Mrs Scott says, 'Don't eat chocolate.'
My teacher's pencil says, 'I am a chocolate.'
My teacher's socks say, 'I am a chocolate.'
Everything in the class says, 'I am a chocolate.'

Gaynor Hartland (9)
Oake & Bradford CP School, Taunton

Limerick

I was teaching in the old school room
When a vampire appeared in the gloom.
So I said, 'Where are you?'
And showered him with glue.
But he took me to his catacomb.

Kelsie Baker (8)
Oldfield Park Junior School, Bath

I Like . . .

I like to see the way the leaves on a tree flutter
in the gentle breeze.

I like to hear the birds twitter and land on
twigs with ease.

I like to smell my nanny cooking Sunday dinner
with green peas.

I like to taste cold ice cream as I leave it to melt
gently in my bowl.

I like to touch the smooth sand as it moulds
round my feet.

I like to look at the gentle pink petals
on a floating lily.

Emma Park (8)
Oldfield Park Junior School, Bath

I Like . . .

I like to see the sea rushing to the rough shore,
I like to hear the rustling sea inside a shell.
I like to smell the honey nectar inside a sweet flower,
I like to taste the glittering honey, sparkling
I like to touch the smooth, silky cats, along the neighbourhood.

Charlotte Rees (9)
Oldfield Park Junior School, Bath

Computers

C omputers are the best
O range background
M iniclip, the best website
P rinting started
U nit found
T aught by the Internet
E xcellent games
R esearch is boring
S o buy one!

Anthony Pestel (10)
Oldfield Park Junior School, Bath

Garfield My Cat

Ginger cat
White belly
Food scoffer
Dog hater
Good fighter
Very contented
Mouse buster
Territory defender.

Philip Durham (10)
Oldfield Park Junior School, Bath

Jake

There once was a man called Jake
Who likes to eat cake
So he bit off a slice
It wasn't very nice
And then he threw it in the lake!

Matthew Arthurs (10)
Oldfield Park Junior School, Bath

If I Had Wings

If I had wings
I would glide gently on the breeze
And sail the fleecy ships.

If I had wings
I would soar over the water
And watch the sea of flying fish.

If I had wings
I would dive through the clouds
And feel the soft breeze hit me.

If I had wings
I would watch the bluebirds fly
And sing their graceful songs.

Rory Colman (7)
Oldfield Park Junior School, Bath

Friends Forever

We've known each other
Since well . . . forever!
I know your mother
And you know mine.
But now distance is parting us
It's not as simple as catching the bus.
I can't believe you're moving to Spain
You'll no longer live just down the lane.
I'll never forget you, we can always write
But I'm saying goodbye because the time is right.

Katy Phillips (10)
Oldfield Park Junior School, Bath

I Want To Be An Astronaut

I want to be an astronaut
And fly up to Mars
To see the shiny moon
And to pass the shooting stars.

I would fly in a rocket
Fly like a golden bird
And see the different things above
There will be nothing to be heard.

I want to be an astronaut
And to find what space is above
Fly through the stars
Whizzing like a roundabout.

I want to spend some holidays
In a shooting rocket
And to see the twinkling stars
To catch a bit of twinkle in my pocket.

Emily Walker (7)
Oldfield Park Junior School, Bath

The Chocolate Factory

There was a chocolate factory
It had a lovely chocolate tree
And there's a lovely smell.
Oh my gosh! It's chocolate gel!
This place is Mr Wonka's
But really he is bonkers!
I ran around with utter glee
Wonka did the same, but bashed into me!

Sophie Gwilt (8)
Oldfield Park Junior School, Bath

The Woman Who Drove Into A Canoe

There was a young lady from Crewe
Who was about to drive into a canoe
When she flew in the river
And cut out her liver
But stuck it back in with some glue!

George Haughton (10)
Oldfield Park Junior School, Bath

Colours

What is red? My bed is red
Where I lay my sleepy head

What is blue? The sky is blue
With the clouds flying through

What is green? A snake is green
Hissing in the beautiful scene

What is orange? The sunset is orange
When I eat my hot porridge

What is yellow? A flower is yellow
What a pretty little fellow

What is black? The night is black
With the glowing eyes from a cat.

Jessica Newman (10)
Oldfield Park Junior School, Bath

Pets

S ooty is my cat
O ff he jumps - off the roof!
O ften he eats Whiskas
T eeth as sharp as knives
Y ou may want this cat.

Verity Bean (10)
Oldfield Park Junior School, Bath

My Limerick

My limerick is cool
But someone thinks I'm a fool,
They sit on a table
With poor little Mabel
Then turned into a ghoul!

Rosanna Louise Todd (9)
Oldfield Park Junior School, Bath

The Man From Greece

There was an old man from Greece,
Who just wanted some peace.
So he went to bed
And hurt his head
But couldn't get rid of his niece.

Rebecca Locke (9)
Oldfield Park Junior School, Bath

There's A Monster Under My Bed

I see shadows on my wall,
I think it is a monster.
I'm scared
I tuck in so he can't get me
Then I realise
It's my shadow!

Kieran Norris (8)
Oldfield Park Junior School, Bath

Hail Storm

It's wicked
It's vicious
It's glittering
It's smashing
It's flashing
It's banging
It's crackling
It's dashing
It's splatting
It's noisy
It's crashing
It's horrible
It's splashing
Now it's hailing
It's cracking
It's breaking
It's hitting
It's smacking
It's slapping
It's punching
It's kicking
It's dropping
It's plopping
It's slopping
It's nasty
It's sly
It's nudging
It's hurting
It's squirting
It's flicking
It's knocking
Suddenly, it stopped!

Megan Doman (8)
Oldfield Park Junior School, Bath

What If?

What if the sun doesn't rise?
What if I forget to get out of bed?
What if my friends have overslept?
What if dinner time doesn't call?
What if my mum doesn't pick me up from school?
What if the sun doesn't go down?
What if I don't do my homework?
What if I didn't sleep?
What if the night was so deep?
What if?

Charlie Bolwell (8)
Oldfield Park Junior School, Bath

Flood

It's runny
It's salty
It's strong
It's dirty
It's rushing
It's mushing
It's crashing
It's rippling
It's splashing.

Stephen Weeks-Dye (8)
Oldfield Park Junior School, Bath

The Pirate

He has a patch upon his eye,
Scared right now, prepare to die.
Sail across the Antarctic Sea
Look out, he's come for me!
He's got me trapped! Someone help!
Save me now before I yelp!

Seb Burvill (11)
Oldfield Park Junior School, Bath

Rats

People are scared of their tails
but they only have them to balance,
they aren't lethal weapons.

They hate rats with red eyes,
Some rabbits have red eyes,
but you hate them, don't you?

They think they're going to bite them,
Hamsters can bite you too!

Apparently they started the plague,
That was the fleas, rats couldn't help carrying them,
it's not like they had shampoo!

Seventy-five percent of the world hates rats
but I think they're brilliant!

Morwenna Harrington (11)
Oldfield Park Junior School, Bath

My Rabbit

My rabbit is called Softie,
He's the best rabbit there could be.
He really loves a hug from me,
I love to hug him too.
He loves to go for a run
He really is loads of fun.
He loves to play
I stroke him every day.
My rabbit is called Softie,
He's the best rabbit there could be!

Sophie Burman (11)
Oldfield Park Junior School, Bath

My Best Friend

My best friend is Tash
She likes to eat bangers and mash!
She is very kind
She's easy to find.
She dances when she's happy
She dances when she's sad.
She's so amazing that's why I'm glad,
She's my best friend!

Jessica Archer (11)
Oldfield Park Junior School, Bath

Fast Cars

My car is very fast
It's kitted up to the max.
It never comes last
It's such a blast.
So take a seat and relax.

Simon Shell (11)
Oldfield Park Junior School, Bath

Lovely Cats

Cats are cuddly,
Cats are cute.
Some are big
Some are minute.
They come in brown, black and white,
Witches' cats are as black as night.
Proudly they prance around the street,
Being friendly to other cats that they meet.
Then when they are tired and need to sleep,
Their owners call them inside, and
Zzzzzzzzzzzzzzzz.

Chloé Chandler (11)
Oldfield Park Junior School, Bath

Dogs, Cats And Mice

Dogs are cute and cuddly,
Cats are small and sweet.
Mice are nasty and ugly,
But what happens when they meet?
The dog will chase the pussy cat,
The mouse will run away,
The owner calls them for their dinner
They'll meet one another!
The dog will eat the cat's food,
The cat will just look and stare.
The mouse will creep into a corner
And nibble his cheese there!

Claire Kingwell (11)
Oldfield Park Junior School, Bath

My Family

My dad plays rugby
I like it too.
My sisters like drawing
I just say, 'Boo!'
My mum is a nurse
I think that's quite good.
My family went on holiday
It was in a wood.
My nan has a dog
His name is Eric,
My grampy has a bad back
His name is Derick.

Now I have introduced you to my family,
Have a good day and live happily.

Emily Doman (10)
Oldfield Park Junior School, Bath

Leeds United

Leeds are the best
They beat Wolves 4 - 1
Now they've started winning
They won't go down to Division One.

Andrew Strange (10)
Oldfield Park Junior School, Bath

My Mum And Nan

My mum is the best
She's pretty,
She rocks the west!
She always does anything I want her to
That's the thing my mum can always do.
My nan is brilliant,
She's worth more than a million.
I love my family and they love me
Thank You God
For making me happy!

Kieran Cox (10)
Oldfield Park Junior School, Bath

Bart Simpson

There was a young boy called Bart,
Who always plays in the dark.
Homer got mad and said,
'You're bad!
I think I'll go and play darts.'

Aaron Kirkwood (10)
Oldfield Park Junior School, Bath

Colours

What is red?
A cap is red
Laying on my bed

What is green?
Grass is green
With flowers in-between.

What is blue?
The sky is blue
In the sky, so true.

What is yellow?
A lemon is yellow
When the juice runs out.

What is pink?
A pig is pink
In the farmyard.

What is grey?
Hair is grey
On a dog.

What is black?
A blackbird is black
In the morning.

Zoe Macey (10)
Oldfield Park Junior School, Bath

I'm A Litter Picker I Bet!

I'm a litter picker I bet
From Bath and North East Somerset
I pick it up through the night and day
Until my hands decide to give way.
I pick up litter on my knees
And I take out plastic bags from the trees.
You'd think I'd be rich, finding money in a ditch
But the most I've found are sixty-three keys!

Ryan Tainton (10)
Oldfield Park Junior School, Bath

Me

Park lover
Sweet eater
Flower liker
Good drawer
Animal lover
Book reader
School liker
Coke drinker.

Gemma Eades (9)
Oldfield Park Junior School, Bath

My Best Friend (Laura)

Animal lover
Friend forgiver
Kind smiler
Hair glitterer
Coke drinker
Funny joker
Good designer
Bike rider
Brilliant wrapper
Food eater
Best writer.

Holly Aldous (10)
Oldfield Park Junior School, Bath

Football Man

Long kicker
Football lover
Excellent passer
Good runner
Fast kicker
Good goalkeeper.

Scott Jardine (10)
Oldfield Park Junior School, Bath

My Cat

Smooth lover
Lazy stretcher
Scratch maker
Stripy miaower
Sneaky purrer
Noisy player.

Jessica Asquith Dagger (10)
Oldfield Park Junior School, Bath

My Dog

Loud barker,
Fast runner,
Slow eater,
Good washer,
Fast licker.

Samuel Blackmore (10)
Oldfield Park Junior School, Bath

My Best Friend (Amy)

Animal lover,
Nice smiler,
Friend forgiver,
Hair shorter,
Fizzy drinker,
Kind thinker,
Funny joker,
Friendly speaker,
Good drawer,
Great advisor,
Fine designer,
Brilliant writer.

Rebecca Wall (9)
Oldfield Park Junior School, Bath

Andy

Football player
TV watcher
Ice cream lover
Cheeky chatter
Sweetie wrapper
Chocolate lover.

Abigail Strange (9)
Oldfield Park Junior School, Bath

Cooking

Food lover
Hand washer
Cake maker
Cake taster
Mess maker
Big eater
Long sleeper.

Emma Oatley (9)
Oldfield Park Junior School, Bath

Beckham

Star kicker
Football lover
Good runner
Excellent passer
Stunning tackler.

Wil Escott (9)
Oldfield Park Junior School, Bath

Spider

Good-crawler
Web-shooter
Good-swinger
Fly-eater
Girl-scarer.

Answer: Spider!

Ross Ashman (10)
Oldfield Park Junior School, Bath

Snowman

Quiet melter
Sun hater
Snow creature
Ice lover
Hat wearer.

Daniel Ashworth (9)
Oldfield Park Junior School, Bath

Monkey

Cheeky climber
Bug eater
Good screamer
Amazing jumper
Fast runner
Good looker
Stunning swinger
Lazy sleeper.

Michael Cook (9)
Oldfield Park Junior School, Bath

Elephant

Huge bulk
Grey hulk
People loader
Tree mower.

Peter Sixsmith (10)
Oldfield Park Junior School, Bath

Mum

Bedroom-tidier
Dirt-hater
Healthy-eater
Light-sleeper.
Who am I?

Emily Tolley (10)
Oldfield Park Junior School, Bath

My Hands

I use my hands to write,
I use my hands to play,
I use my hands to pick up things,
I use my hands every day.

Emma Walker (10)
Oldfield Park Junior School, Bath

Stars

Stars come out at night,
The light is so bright,
Up by the moon,
What an awesome sight.

Chelsea Buchan (9)
Oldfield Park Junior School, Bath

Image Poem

The crack in a windowpane is like . . .
Lightning near a haunted castle
Elevator in Woolworth's
Scar on Harry Potter's head
Pointed fingers of an evil witch
Volcano explosion in New York
A catapult hitting Doulting.

Oliver Crouch (9)
St Aldhelm's CE Primary School, Shepton Mallet

The Crack In A Windowpane Is Like . . .

A star in the misty sky
Lightning striking a tree in the old wood
Harry Potter's scar in a scary room
A spider's web in a light room
A lump of dust in the dark room
A bolt of lightning in the night sky
The hand of a sharp mean wizard in a red room
A golden comet from outer space
A staircase in a haunted mansion
A hurricane slicing through a dusty farm.

Joshua Cawsey (8)
St Aldhelm's CE Primary School, Shepton Mallet

Dear Ocean

Dear Ocean,
What do you hold right at the bottom of you?

I hold the ghostly wreck of the Titanic decaying and rusting,
I hold the shining treasures of Atlantis
And all the magnificent sea creatures.

Isaac Lucksted (9)
St Aldhelm's CE Primary School, Shepton Mallet

Image Poem

The crack in a windowpane looks like:
A piece of dust dangling from a small corner
A falling star out of control
The zigzagged scar that Harry Potter can't get rid of
A snake slithering on the floor
Escalators going up to the Clothes Department
The sharp nails of an evil witch's long finger
A crooked branch of an old tree
Flashing lightning pointed down from a wild sky.

Sophie Porter (9)
St Aldhelm's CE Primary School, Shepton Mallet

Image Poem

The crack in a windowpane is like:
A shooting star hitting the ground making the sky glow
A huge fire from a hot spark
Lightning striking a tree from a black soft cloud
A wizard pointing his fingers at you
Like Harry Potter's scar that is under his hair
Like an escalator in a haunted mansion leading nowhere.

Jordan Saunders (8)
St Aldhelm's CE Primary School, Shepton Mallet

Despair

A lonely tree stands in the garden
Shedding its leaves like an old man losing his hair
A landmark in a desolate land
A single life force yet filled with sorrow
It stands in a blank land
Never to see any other again
Dying slowly
Knowing no love, only pain.

Luke Selwyn-James (11)
St Aldhelm's CE Primary School, Shepton Mallet

My Snow Poem

Snow glows like glitter,
Overwhelming you with beauty,
Shimmering in the distance,
Entrancing you with its reflective shield,
Blinding you with brightness.

Adelle Simik (10)
St Aldhelm's CE Primary School, Shepton Mallet

Marvellous Snow!

Snow gleams like a wizard's stave,
Twinkling with its beauty,
It glows strongly, shimmering sending secret curses above,
Putting you in a trance,
And it sparkles with affection,
Glistens with its jewelled twinkle,
Snow you're so crunchy it's like cornflakes,
And as slushy as melted ice cream.

Paul Willcox (9)
St Aldhelm's CE Primary School, Shepton Mallet

Sun In Space

'Dear Sun in space,
How hot is it up there?'
'I am so hot I could kill thousands if you come too close.'

'Dear Sun in space
Is it lonely up there?'
'Yes, but I get along with Mars.'

'Dear Sun in space
Why are you not hot in winter?'
'Because in the winter I rest.'

Katie Burr (10)
St Aldhelm's CE Primary School, Shepton Mallet

Haiku - My Bad Brother

There were four people,
They're fighting like animals,
They are animals.

Part man, part tiger,
They stand on two feet or four,
Hear them do a roar.

Look at their big teeth,
They are so serious,
They are lost devils.

Adam Earney (10)
St Aldhelm's CE Primary School, Shepton Mallet

Tortoise

I am a tortoise
Once I ate a juicy tomato
Sometimes my master would pat me
I would be able to go inside
I could play in the garden.

But now I have to sit around
Finish my final bit of water
Having a colossal dinner
Watching my master play with a ball.

Soon I will crawl inside my box
Have a enormous yawn
Move a bit
Then start to hibernate.

Lewis Thompson (9)
St Aldhelm's CE Primary School, Shepton Mallet

The River

'Dear River,
Why are you always in such a hurry?'

'Because I like to go so fast that it feels
Like I am skimming across the rocks.'

'Do you have any family?'
'Yes, many streams which are like my children.'

'Where do you lead?'
'The sea.'

Lauren Luxford (11)
St Aldhelm's CE Primary School, Shepton Mallet

Snow

Stepping in the snow is like oozing in marzipan,
A sea of sugar smothering the grass,
Like glowing stars as bright as the sun,
Silver glitter gleaming like cat's eyes.

Freya Doughty (9)
St Aldhelm's CE Primary School, Shepton Mallet

Dear Volcano

Aren't you hot with all that lava?

Yes, very, I wish I could be a mountain
And live in Switzerland then I would keep cool!

Elise Henderson (9)
St Aldhelm's CE Primary School, Shepton Mallet

A Question To You!

Dear Glasses,
Frame do you ever pick on the specs?
Yes because specs are small and I am big.

Do you have a favourite book?
No, but my owner loves all words.

What about a favourite owner?
I like all people but Rolf Harris is my favourite.

Amy Vincent (11)
St Aldhelm's CE Primary School, Shepton Mallet

Dear River,

'Dear River,
Where do you end?'
'I never come to a stop.
I just keep on going and going
Through land and sea.'

'Dear River,
Are you ever lonely?'
'I am often joined by others and I love
Playing with all the wildlife in and around me.'

'Dear River,
Will you ever grow up?'
'One day I will grow up and be called the sea,
Then go back into a river again.'

Becky Holmes (11)
St Aldhelm's CE Primary School, Shepton Mallet

The Wind

The wind
Howls in the night like a ravenous wolf,
It tears through anything in its path,
It whistles tunes randomly in the night,
It silently creeps to catch the last leaf.

Laura Barnes (11)
St Aldhelm's CE Primary School, Shepton Mallet

Curtains Haiku

Behind the window
The curtains hang motionless
Still as time shut down.

George Carey (10)
St Aldhelm's CE Primary School, Shepton Mallet

Snow Dreams

Last night
Something happened
And today our world is like
Shining white pebbles
Washing powder falling from the sky
Sugar drifting from the trees.

Katie Luxford (8)
St Aldhelm's CE Primary School, Shepton Mallet

Freezer

Inside the stainless steel freezer
A frozen chip is playing football with a pea
Like Beckham at the height of his powers.

Jack Hawes-Rowsell (11)
St Aldhelm's CE Primary School, Shepton Mallet

The Hot Tub

The warm bubbly hot tub,
Hot and steamy,
Eating lollies in the hot tub,
Hot and boiling,
On the beds in the sauna,
Top it up with more water,
Towels to dry yourself when you get out,
Underneath the water jets are spraying out bubbles,
Bubbles still bubbling.

Catherine Reakes (11)
St Aldhelm's CE Primary School, Shepton Mallet

The Raging Sea

Rushing white horses galloping along,
On foamy white waves fast and strong.

Great white whale diving in and out,
Throwing out fountains from its spout.

Crashing and collapsing against the rocks,
While thunder and lightning strikes down like a shock.

Frogfish huddling on the seabed,
Grazing while sharks swim above their heads.

Hannah Nicholls (11)
St Aldhelm's CE Primary School, Shepton Mallet

I Am

I am a wave in the deep blue sea crashing against the sand,
In the summer, welcoming and slippery like an ice cream,
Playing with my mates every Wednesday afternoon,
I am cold and icy and rough in the winter,
I crash against the sand like my mates,
They usually go further than me.

Luke Harris (8)
St Aldhelm's CE Primary School, Shepton Mallet

Dear Titanic

Dear Titanic,
When you saw the iceberg, how did you feel?
I was scared that I would let everyone down.

How did you feel when you started to sink?
I started to shiver so I knew something was wrong.

Who do you miss the most?
I miss them all but most of them lay beside me.

Rhiannon Haskins (11)
St Aldhelm's CE Primary School, Shepton Mallet

River

'Dear River,
Why do you rush past me?'
'I'm hurrying to see the sea.'

'Where do you end?'
'I never end, I keep going.'

'How do you spread your streams?'
'The clouds cry and I grow.'

Stacey Smith (10)
St Aldhelm's CE Primary School, Shepton Mallet

Mr Volcano

What's it like being filled with hot lava?
Lovely and bubbly I feel like I'm in a hot tub,
Mr Volcano what is your favourite colour?
Orange of course it's my mobile network
Sir Volcano what time do you erupt?
Any time you wish majesty,
Master Volcano what excites you?
Hot spicy curry with chilli sauce and two splashes of smoke.

Chay Warren (10)
St Aldhelm's CE Primary School, Shepton Mallet

I'm A Bedroom

I'm a bedroom
Smelling of deodorant
With the floor a tip.
The window open,
Giving me goose pimples.
The corners of me have spiders in them
I'm collecting dust,
I wish I had a wash,
There is no point,
I'm always dirty,
I smell like petrol,
Like rats breath and dust,
With a television that hadn't been
Used since 1935.

Alex Gregory (11)
St Aldhelm's CE Primary School, Shepton Mallet

The Image Of A Crack

The crack in a window is like:
The scar on Harry Potter's head
A bolt of lightning from a misty cloud
A glowing star in the night sky
An earthquake in middle Earth
A shooting star in the night sky falling
The sharp nails of an ugly hag
The crooked side of an escalator
A firework exploding in the dusky night.

John Moulton (8)
St Aldhelm's CE Primary School, Shepton Mallet

Dear Sun

'Dear Sun,
Why don't you come out at night?'
'The thought of it breaks my heart.'

'Why are you so yellow and bright?'
'I have a heart of gold.'

'What do you do at night?'
'I send the moon for a night light.'

Sarah Ford (10)
St Aldhelm's CE Primary School, Shepton Mallet

I'm Small

I'm small
As small as a pebble on the beach,
As small as a leaf from the largest tree.

I'm tiny
I am a caterpillar on a twig on the ground,
I am a miniature black beetle scurrying across the grass.

I'm microscopic
I feel like a baby ant in my cocoon,
I feel like a speck of dust in someone's eye,
Will I ever be found?

Laurie Pillinger (9)
St Aldhelm's CE Primary School, Shepton Mallet

Cracks

The crack in the windowpane looks like . . .
A star in a distant constellation,
A bolt of lightning in the sky,
A staircase that goes nowhere,
A snowflake with no friends,
The scar that Harry Potter is cursed with.

Sam Garbett (9)
St Aldhelm's CE Primary School, Shepton Mallet

Tiger

A tiger has claws
and very big paws,
She lives in the jungle
and rolls and tumbles.

Tiger, tiger with bright green eyes,
in bright, hot sun she lies.

A tiger roars
and lies on floors,
She often catches prey
so you should stay away.

Tiger, tiger with bright green eyes,
in bright, hot sun she lies.

The tiger has bold, black stripes,
but you'd better watch out because she will bite,
She never runs out of food,
her hunting is exceptionally good.

Tiger, tiger with bright green eyes,
in bright, hot sun she lies.

Naomi Stearn (10)
St John's CE VA Primary School, Midsomer Norton

Tiger

The tiger,
Very fast at getting its prey,
Has sharp teeth,
Has black stripes over orange,
Good at hiding in grass,
Good at seeing and hearing,
Good sense of smell,
Very good at sneaking up to its prey.
Dangerous tiger.

Gareth Fear (10)
St John's CE VA Primary School, Midsomer Norton

I Had A Dream

I had a dream
about whipped cream,
covered with cherries and ice.

I picked up my spoon,
took a mouthful,
and umm . . . it was nice!

I had a dream
about a stream
of lovely chocolate sauce.

I picked up my spoon,
took a mouthful and umm . . . a scrumptious main course!

I had a dream
about ice cream,
frozen in a tub.

I picked up my spoon,
took a mouthful,
and umm . . . great grub!

Daniel McCarthy (10)
St John's CE VA Primary School, Midsomer Norton

Living Lizard

Lizard living,
living in the jungle,
small and scary,
claws crawling up trees,
changes colour,
camouflaged,
waits patiently
for its dinner.

Taylor Young (10)
St John's CE VA Primary School, Midsomer Norton

Pollution

Pollution has had its birth,
Its mother being technology
A new factory has been opened.

Pollution has begun to grow
It has new helpers cars,
Its new friend has a gracious child,
Carbon dioxide.

Pollution grows more and more,
It becomes a huntsman,
Its prey being small animals,
It still thrives on death.

It is time, pollution has its children,
Gases and contaminants poison water and the environment,
Now its children have children.
Is that what you wanted, death?

Who's to blame? Yourself.
Did you expect to revolutionise Earth without consequences?
Because if you did, instead of doing that, you're killing
Earth . . . maybe.
What a shame, it's all down to you, make a change!

Benjamin Davis (11)
St John's CE VA Primary School, Midsomer Norton

Lightning

Lightning's frightening,
Very, very frightening,
It clashes hard and it roars *loud.*
It's terrifying and electrifying,
Earth-shaking and *window-shattering.*
Striking hard, fast, its powers in its wake.
Destroying all around, the lightning stops with a massive, shocking
Flash!

Liam Snow (11)
St John's CE VA Primary School, Midsomer Norton

Lions In Action

Lion in the sun
protecting its family,
Lion in the sun
relaxing in its habitat,
Lion in the sun
sharpening its teeth,
Lion in the sun
eating others around!
Lion in the sun
Dangerously hunting,
Lion in the sun
tearing and shredding,
Lion in the sun
clawing at its mane,
Lion in the sun
running faster and faster,
Lion in the sun,
bang! It's in agony.

What shall I do?

Tamsin Perry (10)
St John's CE VA Primary School, Midsomer Norton

The Baboon

Went to the zoo, saw a baboon,
It has a colourful nose,
It walked on four legs,
It had a long tail,
It loved peanuts and vegetables,
It had a face like a dog,
It had sharp teeth,
It should live in the jungle!

Victoria Vine (10)
St John's CE VA Primary School, Midsomer Norton

Holidays

Happy people eating food,
Arcades get you in the mood,
Stay up late playing games,
Lots of ice cream stains.

Holidays, holidays are lots of fun,
under the bright, hot sun!

On the beach with buckets and spades,
All our sunhats begin to fade.
Splashing and playing in the ocean,
Remember to put on lots of suntan lotion.

Holidays, holidays are lots of fun,
under the bright, hot sun!

Children watching Punch and Judy,
Holidays when no one gets moody.
Spending money on nice things,
Watching the birds with golden wings.

Holidays, holidays are lots of fun,
under the bright, hot sun!

Amelia Collins (10)
St John's CE VA Primary School, Midsomer Norton

Snakes

Sliding, slimy snakes slither along the ground,
smooth, squashy snakes slide through the grass.
Camouflaged so much no one can see them eat
tiny, little animals and nibble little feet.

Some are poisonous from their bites,
some are long and give you frights.
There are wild snakes, grass snakes, some really heavy,
some are plain and some are stripy.

Liam Horler (10)
St John's CE VA Primary School, Midsomer Norton

The Hippopotamus

Hippopotamus is born,
recent life has struck.
Hippopotamus is idle,
protected by its mother.
Hippopotamus gets hungry,
its mother feeds it.
Hippopotamus gets more muscle,
grows into an adult.
Hippopotamus hears a gunshot,
wakes up in a cage.

Becky Evans (11)
St John's CE VA Primary School, Midsomer Norton

My Holiday

I'm packing for my holiday,
I'm ever so excited,
I can imagine
Sun, sea, sand and fun,
We're ready to go!
I can feel the heat
Beneath my feet,
Burning sand,
Scorching sun,
Roaring waves on the beach
So I play games!
I watch the sunset
From my balcony,
I think to myself,
This is a perfect holiday.

Rachel Davies (11)
St John's CE VA Primary School, Midsomer Norton

In Danger

Sneaking through the emerald jungle,
the shimmering sun beating down.
Admired by its rich, colourful patterns,
moving swiftly through the rustling grass.
But wait, the snake is in danger,
poachers are out to kill!
Could this be the end?
Suddenly a gunshot,
the snake is lifeless . . .

Jodie Fear (11)
St John's CE VA Primary School, Midsomer Norton

The Spider Hunting For Its Prey

A big spider hunting for its prey,
creeping closer,
prey sitting there unaware.
The spider sees it from quite a distance,
it jumps,
its hairy, strong legs wrestle its prey.
It injects its poison,
food arrives,
death comes.

Liam Hall (10)
St John's CE VA Primary School, Midsomer Norton

Unicorns

Intelligent creatures use their magic powers,
With long, thick, slightly crimped mane and tail, show elegance.
A crystal white, soft and warm coat and a twirling glass horn.
Hooves thunder on the moist ground as they gallop through
rich, green fields.
Magnificent unicorns!

Lila Ayres (11)
St John's CE VA Primary School, Midsomer Norton

Families

Families look after each other,
Families scare each other,
Families read to each other,
Families play with each other,
Families mess around with each other,
Families laugh with each other,
Families watch television with each other,
Families argue with each other,
Families shout at each other,
Families *love each other.*

Rebekah Vicary (10)
St John's CE VA Primary School, Midsomer Norton

Cat

Cat in the garden
jumping up and down
catching flies,
pounces on birds,
happy, playful cat.

Cat in the house
sitting by the fire
stroked by its owner,
purring more and more,
relaxed, content cat.

Cat in the garden,
daily scrap with the cat next door,
dodging the dog,
runs to the field,
puffing, panting, sick cat.

Esther Bunney (10)
St John's CE VA Primary School, Midsomer Norton

Friends

Have you ever had the perfect friend,
Or just a friend that drives you round the bend?
All there is, is the perfect touch,
These are the people we love so much.

Your friend cares for you,
And will always be there for you.
You will always be able to trust them,
And always rely on them.

Have you ever had the perfect friend,
Or just a friend that drives you round the bend?
All they need is the perfect touch,
These are the people we love so much.

Ashley Griffiths-Thorn (10)
St John's CE VA Primary School, Midsomer Norton

The Slime

There's a certain slime
That goes round committing crime!
It goes round wasting time!
It looks suspiciously like lime!

When it creates grief,
The slime makes it very brief!
People say it lives on a reef!
The slime has two sharp teeth!

He's very slow
But delivers a fatal blow!
People have seen the slime glow!
On the reef he lives in a burrow!

There's a certain slime
That goes round committing crime!
It goes round wasting time!
It looks suspiciously like lime!

Max Hillman (11)
St John's CE VA Primary School, Midsomer Norton

My Magic Box

(Based on 'Magic Box' by Kit Wright)

I will put in my magic box . . .
a fly in a swamp,
a dragon making a stomp,
and elephant in a candyfloss lump.

I will put in my magic box . . .
a bang from a firework's light,
an aeroplane on a one-way flight,
a spark from Jesus' flash on a winter's night.

I will put in my magic box . . .
a baby in her tiny cot,
an egg in a frying pot,
a man in a sailing yacht.

I will put in my magic box . . .
a 13th month and an unknown name,
a cowboy on a fly who never came.
a footballer without his only game.

I will fly in my magic box . . .
to the rainbow's side,
and everyone helps me decide
to fly on my box and go for a glide.

Joseph Cottle (7)
St John's CE VA Primary School, Midsomer Norton

In My Darkest Hour

In my darkest hour, dreams turned to nightmares,
In my darkest hour, civilisation began to tear.
In my darkest hour, zombies rose from the dead,
In my darkest hour, all angels fled,
In my darkest hour, the sun went out.
In my darkest hour, vampires rose up and flew about.
In my darkest hour, my blood bank lost control,
In my darkest hour, the world began to roll.

James Iley Hazelgrove (10)
St John's CE VA Primary School, Midsomer Norton

The Magic Box

(Based on 'Magic Box' by Kit Wright)

I will put in the box . . .
A swish of a sail,
A spark from the Fire of London,
A twinkle from the Bethlehem star.

I will put in the box . . .
A glimpse of a firework,
A sprinkle from hundreds and thousands,
A raindrop from a shower of rain.

I will put in the box . . .
A bullet from the First World War,
A piece of happiness to win 1,000,000 pounds on 'Who Wants to be a Millionaire?'
A feather from a baby bird.

I will put in the box . . .
A number from the first piece of maths,
A drop of blood from the first patient.
A staple from the first thing put on the wall.

My box is fashioned with iron, silk and wood,
With hearts stuck on the lid,
And dreams tucked away in the corners.
The hearts are the cards from Valentine's Day.

I shall dance in my box till the sun will rise,
I shall take it to school and leave it all day,
And at the end of the week, it will float away.

Willow Wyatt (7)
St John's CE VA Primary School, Midsomer Norton

Fireworks

See fireworks
rocket skywards
as loud as a herd of elephants,
as high as the Eiffel Tower,
as colourful as a flower bed.
The smell of a bonfire
as enjoyable as a roller coaster,
metallic and speckled like an egg,
it's like glitter falling from the sky.
Just like magic powder falling
and vanishing into thin air
and as sparkling as a star.

Smell fireworks
as they fly
like birds in the air
as swiftly a white dove.

Feel fireworks,
rough like a rock,
hard and pointed,
dusty to touch.

Hear fireworks
in the air, as they whistle
like a warden in a station
a deafening screech.

Connor Evans (11)
St John's CE VA Primary School, Midsomer Norton

What Is Yellow?

Yellow is the sun
blazing in the sky.
Yellow is canaries
flying high.
Flapping parrots
floating in the sky,
popping out to say
bye-bye!
Fresh, yummy lemons
gleaming in the sun,
round like a melon
growing in the sun.
Floating autumn leaves
blowing in the wind,
golden crowns
from the heads of kings.

Charlotte Laing (8)
St John's CE VA Primary School, Midsomer Norton

Clash

Humpty Dumpty sat on the wall,
Humpty Dumpty had a great fall,
Spiderman, Spiderman,
He does whatever a spider can,
'Hey, what are you doing in my poem?'
And all the king's horses and all the king's men
Couldn't put Humpty together again,
Catches things just like flies,
Watch out here comes Spiderman,
'Hey you smell of pies.'

Marlo Sawyer (11)
St John's CE VA Primary School, Midsomer Norton

Through That Door

Through that door
is a waterfall,
big and loud,
so, so tall.
Flowers called lilies,
bright like the sun.
Soft fluffy bunnies,
run, run, run.

Olivia Webster (8)
St John's CE VA Primary School, Midsomer Norton

The Crab

A shore creeper
A sand digger
A rock hider
A suit of armour
A claw slasher
A rock pool dweller
A tough crustacean
A part of the beach.

Ben Wilshire (11)
St John's CE VA Primary School, Midsomer Norton

What Is White?

Cold as icicles,
Fresh as spring,
Gentle sky
Like silver wings.
Fresh as ice cream,
Cold as snow,
Frozen snowflakes,
Cheeks will glow.

Demelza Clegg (7)
St John's CE VA Primary School, Midsomer Norton

Sleeping Beauty

S leeping for 100 years,
L onely people cried with tears,
E veryone fell to the ground,
E verlasting, all year round.
P eople slept along with her,
I myself have heard,
N othing moved in the castle,
G oing nowhere for a while.

B ut the fairies of her land
E ver changing from hand to hand,
A prince came along and woke her with a kiss,
U nder a spell it broke with this,
T o their wedding they went,
Y ou know how much they spent.

Rebecca Killey (10)
St John's CE VA Primary School, Midsomer Norton

The Cat

A night prowler
A fence jumper
A field hunter
A wall crawler
A food scavenger
A clawed beast
A cautious animal
A day sleeper
A dangerous pouncer
A camouflaged leaper.

Matthew Brimble (10)
St John's CE VA Primary School, Midsomer Norton

Dinosaur

I was walking through the forest
I looked up through the trees,
There was a dinosaur
'Please don't eat me, please!'

It looked at me,
Eyes beady and wide,
It opened up its mouth
And now I'm inside!

Katie Hutton (11)
St John's CE VA Primary School, Midsomer Norton

Three Little Pigs

T rying to get out of trouble
H urrying to build a house,
E at the three little pigs.

T rying to get them,
H urrying against time,
R acing against the wolf,
E ating his way through,
E scaping from the big, bad wolf.

L icking his lips,
I nvestigating where the pigs went,
T aking them away,
T he time is running out,
L aughing,
E ating them.

P uffing and coughing through,
I n their houses,
G etting his way through
S houting for help.

Chernenko Marinay (10)
St John's CE VA Primary School, Midsomer Norton

Spring Flowers

See spring flowers
shoot up,
yellow as a lemon,
orange as orange paint,
purple as a plum.

Smell spring flowers,
soft as a seashell,
silky as my slippers.

Spring flowers
are beautiful.

Daniella Marchment (8)
St John's CE VA Primary School, Midsomer Norton

Rapunzel

Locked up in a tower so tall,
waiting for Mr Right to call,
she survived on milk and cookies for tea,
she missed the world that she couldn't see.
The love of her life came and looked up,
Rapunzel yelled for help!
He said, 'Let down your hair so fair
and I will climb up your hair.
I'll save your life
with my knife
and we will get married tonight.'
He climbed her hair and she was safe
and they lived together for ever!

Sam Lang (11)
St John's CE VA Primary School, Midsomer Norton

Rapunzel

R apunzel is really beautiful,
A ppearing in the street,
P ink flared out dress,
U nable to go out,
N asty, cruel customer,
Z ipping for freedom,
E merald necklace round her neck,
L ips shining in the light.

Demi Lane (10)
St John's CE VA Primary School, Midsomer Norton

Through That Door

Through that door
is a tower so tall
with animals gathered
if you sit under a tree
you hear the wind call
'How are you?'
'I am fine'
'Who are you,
A friend of mine?'

Through that door
there is a big, big moor
it is so big, it's bigger than the floor
it's as green as a pear
if you hug it you will see
an invisible baby bumblebee.

Grace Collins (7)
St John's CE VA Primary School, Midsomer Norton

Walking In The Woods

Walking, walking in the woods,
Riding Hood with lots of puds
For her granny,
She's very funny!
Walking in the woods.

Walking, walking in the woods
Still with her puds,
'Boo!' A wolf jumps out,
And gives her a fright,
Walking in the woods.

Walking, walking in the woods,
And still with her puds,
'Where are you going?' the wolf asks,
'I'm going to my granny's' and she passes,
Walking in the woods.

Walking, walking in the woods,
She's still, still with her puds,
'Wait!' the wolf cries,
Red Riding Hood sighs,
Walking in the woods.

Walking, walking in the woods,
And still, still with her puds,
The sly wolf says, 'I know a short cut.'
She looks along the pathway, she sees her granny in her hut,
Walking in the woods.

Walking, walking in the woods,
She gives her the puds,
The wolf didn't meet her
To eat her,
Walking in the woods.

Megan Thomas (10)
St John's CE VA Primary School, Midsomer Norton

Cinderella

C inderella cleans the floor,
I n despair she waits for more,
N o food, no drink,
D evastated, she can't think,
E very morning when she awakes,
R inging of the bell, tower shakes,
E very knee bows, the prince is here,
L ass, love, you'll go to the ball, come now, dear,
L ove, care and laughter,
A nd wishing they will live happily ever after.

Bethany Williams (11)
St John's CE VA Primary School, Midsomer Norton

Rain Poem

Plip plop,
Rain's dropped.
Dripping through clouds,
Soggy clothes cling,
Catch the raindrops on the windows,
Thunder enjoys trees falling,
Clouds are ghosts,
Wind takes umbrellas,
Rain like my shadow,
Puddles are mirrors,
I see a shrivelled orange,
Drip, drop, can't stop.
And suddenly, sun springs from cold,
Ducks swim in reflective water,
Grass squelching, I don't care,
I'm leaping through puddles,
Sun is the twinkling in my mum's eyes.

Rebecca Davies (8)
St Martin's Garden Primary School, Bath

The Gazelle's Last Day

Slowly walking through the corn field,
Faster, faster, quicker, quicker,
Sprinting through the long, green grass,
You are so very fast.
Gaining, gaining, nearly there,
You're clawing at the gazelle's feet.
Scrap, fall, crash down dead,
Oh dear, too bad, you're dinner tonight.
Slowly walking through the corn field,
Getting faster, faster, faster,
Now that you are in a hurry,
You are going at quite a pace.
Drop the gazelle in your den,
Walk in slowly, now you can rest.
Young ones take the first few bites,
They slowly open the flesh up
So you can have your dinner.
Ripping the flesh from your mighty catch,
Crunching, munching up the food.
Now its time to go to bed,
Goodnight, farewell, another day over and done.

Sam Vinall (9)
St Martin's Garden Primary School, Bath

The Big Black Bull

The big black bull who lives in Spain,
Is scary, ferocious and fierce,
He has two horns that can cause much pain,
And would give you lots of tears,
The big black bull wants to be free,
He wants to jump and run,
He is dangerous and angry,
But all he wants is fun.

Ibrahim Qazi (8)
St Martin's Garden Primary School, Bath

African Ostrich

A n ostrich is really tall
F riendly, well most of the time,
R unning very, very fast,
I t lives in the sandy wastes. Their
C laws are really strong,
A nd extremely sharp.
N orthern ostriches are my favourite.

O ver the
S and he runs
T owards the land.
R unning faster, faster
I n-between the tall trees.
C ould stop but doesn't
H ungry, really hungry, looking for his prey,
E xtremely hungry now, a nice
S nake would do.

Conner Holmes (9)
St Martin's Garden Primary School, Bath

The Snake Poem

A snake is as slippery as a slug,
It slithers through the sand,
Its head is shaped like a hose,
Its eyes are as sharp as cats'.
I wander through the gloomy wood,
Looking for the snake,
I hide, watching, waiting for an hour,
Waiting for the snake to come,
I jump out of the bush and there it is!
The snake is slithering towards me!
I scream, I shout, I shiver and run away,
But the snake slides after me.
I rush away, sprinting towards home,
Hoping he won't follow.

Sean Barbieri (9)
St Martin's Garden Primary School, Bath

Dark Rain

Pillars smashing onto pavements,
Spiky bats biting my nose,
Ghostly trees whistle to each other,
Spheres of fear take over Bath,
Black, lumpy whales float across a sky,
Thunder's mad,
All ferrets hide in cracks,
Spiders tickle toes when all asleep,
But then the thunder disappears,
Ferrets come sneaking out of cracks,
Bats rush away,
Trees come back to life,
Spheres of fear crack,
Black whales fall from the clouds and die,
Spiders crawl into fields.

Cobi Maynard (7)
St Martin's Garden Primary School, Bath

A Lonely Play Time

Sitting on the patio
Watching my best friend
Playing rounders
I wish I could be there
Playing with them.
All alone
By myself.
Suddenly the bell rings,
Slowly my wheels turn
Towards the classroom I go
Silently back to class.
My friend says sorry.

Emily Humphries (9)
St Martin's Garden Primary School, Bath

The Cock Of The Rocks

The cock of the rocks is a musical bird
that sings like Heaven's trumpet.
This bird lives in South America, they dance on grassy plains.
The bird shows off to females so they can mate each year.
This bird's so beautiful humans come nowhere near.
The males dance in beautiful clusters,
and when finished their amazing dance, they bask in golden glory.

Moussa Al Harthy (9)
St Martin's Garden Primary School, Bath

The Sea Turtle

I once saw a sea turtle down at the beach,
I wanted to catch it but it was out of my reach.
It slid into the sea, then it swam off happily.
The sea turtle must be happy swimming through the deep blue sea,
Oh how I wish it was me.

Rebecca Quinlan (9)
St Martin's Garden Primary School, Bath

The Fire Of London

Burning, burning, burning quickly
Run, run, run, run fast.
Quickly, quickly the fire is spreading
I don't know what to do.
But I will try with buckets of water,
Buckets of water
Yes, yes, with buckets of water,
That's it, buckets of water,
That's the trick.

Charlie Bright (7)
St Martin's Garden Primary School, Bath

Rain

It is raining fiercely
Hoods are up
Umbrellas are up
Car windscreen wipers are waving
It's noisy on the rooftops
Fresh to taste
Wet play!
Ponds leaking
Reflections in water.

Then suddenly
The hot sun appears
Hoods down
Cars dry
Sun shining in the windows
Children running
Out to play
Ponds normal
Reflections fading.

Leah McDonagh (8)
St Martin's Garden Primary School, Bath

The Sea

Seagulls in the air,
Seagulls everywhere.
Whales splashing in the sea,
Dolphins jumping over me.
Crabs eating seaweed.
Sharks chasing fish.

Zahria Laing (7)
St Martin's Garden Primary School, Bath

Rain

Dark sky,
Wind blowing,
Wet play,
Grey clouds,
Puddles overflowing,
Shiny roads,
Slippery paths,
Mud all slimy,
Umbrellas up.

But then,
Clouds disappearing,
Rainbows colourful,
Umbrellas down,
Water drying up,
Roads clearing,
Sky blue,
Kids and grown ups
Coming out.
Play time!

Carey Mottram (8)
St Martin's Garden Primary School, Bath

Rain

Wet play,
Can't sunbathe,
Huge drips,
Cold, wet rain
Sounds like
Bacon frying.

Then suddenly
The sun breaks through,
Sunglasses on,
Raincoats off,
Wellies off,
Sunbathe!

Aaron Shaw (8)
St Martin's Garden Primary School, Bath

Rain

Wet play,
Children upset,
Can't play,
Umbrellas are up,
Rain falling,
Children crying,
Wellies on,
No sun,
Rain splattering,
Raincoats on,
Hoods up,
Sounds like
Bacon sizzling,
Puddles growing,
Babies wailing,
Parents working hard!
Streams flowing.

Then suddenly
Clouds disappearing,
Rainbows appearing,
Sun shining through,
Play time,
Children shouting,
Sky was grey,
Now blue,
White clouds,
Children playing,
Dogs in parks,
No more rain!

Aisha Fenton (7)
St Martin's Garden Primary School, Bath

Place Of Mind

I looked in a place where I couldn't be seen,
No monsters, no strangers, nowhere anyone had been.
I sat on the air which was as cold as ice,
And looked all around, it was not very nice.

There was grey, there were shadows, all sunken in mist,
There was no love, no hope, not even a wish.
I stood up and walked on, for miles in an hour,
Still no one, still nothing, but bitter devour

Then all of a sudden a woman in black
Came walking towards me, I tried to stand back.
She just carried on walking and walking the air,
She didn't look at me once, like I just wasn't there.

More shapes came as well except they were flowers,
Flowers and gravestones so black and so sour.
The picture came clear but the woman just sat,
Just waited for wishes and dreams to come back.

I walked forwards to ask her what this was about,
But never got closer just pushed further out.
She shouted and cried as she flicked her black hair,
And she aged every second to my sad despair.

Then all of a sudden, she turned into smoke,
So large and distinctive, it made me start to choke.

I walked to the place where the woman had cried,
And saw a new gravestone . . .

She had, in fact, died.

Rosie Collington (10)
St Mary's CE Primary School, Bridgwater

A Winter Haiku Poem

Snowflakes fall through snow
Spreading bits of white glitter
In the winter night.

Amy Boobyer (10)
St Mary's CE Primary School, Bridgwater

My Family

Hi I'm Jess,
I'm 9, soon to be 10.

Then there's Becky, my sister,
7, soon to be 8.
She loves football,
A sniff of air and she's out.

Next it's my other sister, Pip,
Boss of the house,
3, soon to be 4.

Then my mum,
She's cuddly and kind,
And hates mess.

My dad,
Bald and funny.
(But his jokes aren't.)

Nana,
She has a box full of sweets
And by the end of the day they're gone.
(Yum.)

Finally my grandma and grandad
They always have sweets
And we are allowed to play ball in the kitchen.

Jessica Garland (9)
St Nicholas' Chantry CE School, Clevedon

People

People are happy,
People are sad,
People feel good and people feel bad,
Some people smile and others frown,
Some are chubby and some are thin as well.
But even though we are not the same,
We are all good in our very own way.

Rebecca Hawley (9)
St Nicholas' Chantry CE School, Clevedon

The Five Senses

The lips are made to taste
Apple crumble and apple pie.

The nose is made to smell
The perfume of colourful
Lovely flowers.

The hands are made to feel
The lovely smoothness of
Gold and shiny silver.

The ears are made to hear
The humming sound of
A graceful bird's singing.

The eyes are made to see
The beauty of the
Shimmering ocean.

Polly Tucker (7)
St Nicholas' Chantry CE School, Clevedon

The Wind

The wind,
whistling through my ears
never stopping
and never having a rest.

The wind,
travels everywhere
to the north, south,
east and west.

The wind,
no one can see it
only feel and hear it
and you should always
treat the wind as a guest.

Stephanie Parsons (11)
St Nicholas' Chantry CE School, Clevedon

Winter Is The Time . . .

Winter is the time . . .
When the mornings are freezing,
And frost lies on the ground.

Winter is the time . . .
When footprints are made,
And imprinted in the snow.

Winter is the time . . .
When the snow is cold and crisp,
And the wind is blowing wildly.

Winter is the time . . .
When the trees are bare,
And branches sway in the wind.

Winter is the time . . .
When the evenings are warm and cosy,
With a roaring fire and a steaming mug of chocolate,
I never want those winter days to end.

Ella Miller (8)
St Nicholas' Chantry CE School, Clevedon

Pocket Elephant

Pocket elephant, imagine that, wouldn't that be great?
He'd be sitting in your pocket, just like a real mate.
He would sit in there all day, you could take him to school,
You could name him anything you like, you could name him Paul.
You could keep him in your pocket while you went out for lunch,
You could sit him on the table and give him peanuts to munch.
You could keep him in your pocket when you went to do your sport,
He could be your team mascot when you were on the tennis court.
And when you're feeling sad and blue,
Your pocket elephant would be there too,
Make sure you take care,
Otherwise your pocket elephant won't be there.

Hollie Youde (9)
St Nicholas' Chantry CE School, Clevedon

Once Upon A Rhyme

School, school is a place for us all
With smelly toilets and writing on the wall.
Plenty of reading and writing to be done
But there is also time to have some fun.

I have a teacher so kind and nice,
She is always there to give advice,
We sit on the carpet ready to learn,
Waiting patiently to have a turn.

A ring and a ding, that is the sound,
The boys and girls go to the playground.
Girls are skipping and jumping,
The boys are kicking and bumping.

Back to the classroom with books and toys,
Must be quiet without any noise,
Out with your pencils, ready to go,
Some children fast, some children slow.

Ben Capern (7)
St Nicholas' Chantry CE School, Clevedon

Magic

Something funny happens
on our classroom desks,
our rulers disappear
and pencils develop legs.

It never happens when we're there
only when we're not,
maybe we'll disappear
with pencils and the lot!

Maybe this will stop
by magic far away
done by a wizard called 'Teacher'
who will force the magic astray.

Amy Snow (9)
St Nicholas' Chantry CE School, Clevedon

My Garden

My garden is the place for me
Sitting under an apple tree
The sun is shining down from above
With plants and flowers, that's what I love.

Oh God's nature big or small
I'm just so fascinated by them all
Little insects creeping round
Up in trees and on the ground.

A spider that is black and hairy
It creeps and crawls and looks so scary
As I'm digging in the ground
A pink fat worm is what I've found.

From a little tiny seed
Grew a green enormous weed
With an almighty tug and pull
Now my black bag is nearly full.

Planting bulbs is so much fun
Another job in the garden done
Cut the grass short and neat
Now my friends are in for a treat.

Jamie Capern (9)
St Nicholas' Chantry CE School, Clevedon

Happy Thought

The world
Is so full of
A number of things,
I'm sure we all are as happy as kings
When we play nicely with other people,
So let's enjoy the lovely things
Of the world.

Muirne Cunning (7)
St Nicholas' Chantry CE School, Clevedon

Which Witch Is Which?

They fly on high,
Swooping down from the sky,
Oh, those cackling, growling witches.

The first with her warty nose
And cobwebs everywhere!
Known as Spike
She smells of a dead rose.

The second and third oh my word!
All their creepy,
Scary cats purred.
They're twins, but are as silent as falling pins.

Now there's the fourth, big and round,
Not a rat, but a pet hound
Sitting on the end of her broom.

And at last, number five
Hangs upside down,
Showing the others a double flip zoom . . .

And with a swish of their cloaks, all in black
The crackling, growing witches fly away
From you and I

But,
Which witch is which?
Ha! Ha! Ha!

Frankie Archer (9)
St Nicholas' Chantry CE School, Clevedon

Peace

Peace is colourful,
It smells like a big blossom tree.
Peace tastes like strawberry ice cream,
It sounds like the most beautiful music
It feels like a very soft teddy bear
Peace lives in the bottom of your heart.

Jennifer Taylor (9)
St Nicholas' Chantry CE School, Clevedon

The Iliad II

It was a very long war,
Ten years fighting.
Outside the walls of Troy
Lay the Greeks' camp.

Helen, taken prisoner by the Trojans,
Because Paris liked her.
But Helen was married to Menelaus
So the war started.

Slow to move and heavy the armour,
Weapons made from iron,
Deadly fighting.
Helen would rather die
Than be the cause of the war.

Jack Bradbrook (8)
St Nicholas' Chantry CE School, Clevedon

Friends

If I had a best friend
She would always have to lend
If I had a best friend
She would not drive me round the bend
If I had a best friend
I would like her to the end
I have a best friend
I like her best
I like her more
Than all the rest
She is the greatest
She is the best
She is my friend
Better than all the rest.

Maisie Neath (8)
St Nicholas' Chantry CE School, Clevedon

Number Poem

When I was 4
I learned to open the door.

When I was 5
I learned to dive.

When I was 6
I picked up sticks.

When I was 7
I went to Devon.

When I was 8
I found a mate.

When I was 9
I learned to rhyme.

When I was 10
I found a den.

When I was 11
I went to Heaven.

Liam Richards (7)
St Nicholas' Chantry CE School, Clevedon

Opportunity

O pen the spacecraft door
P ositive brains bubbling non-stop
P roblems flying on swift wings
O pportunity is in the air
R aging problems in the air
T ransport moving gently round Mars
U nknown places in space
N on-stop robot working hard
I nstant work round this planet
T ransport running round the planet working hard
Y et using their brains to work out problems.

Kayleigh Fountain (10)
St Nicholas' Chantry CE School, Clevedon

If The World Was Made Of Sweets

If the world was made of sweets,
Houses of gingerbread.
If the world was made of sweets,
Icing sugar in our bed.

If the world was made of sweets,
Polos for the car wheels.
If the world was made of sweets,
Jelly Tots for cotton reels.

If the world was made of sweets,
Clouds made out of candyfloss.
If the world was made of sweets,
Melted chocolate raindrops.

If the world was made of sweets,
We would never starve.

Tara Fortune (8)
St Nicholas' Chantry CE School, Clevedon

Chocolate

How I love chocolate so much
My mouth waters when I see it.
It comes in all different shapes, what fun
And I love it when it melts on my tongue.
I love *chocolate.*

Georgia Longstaff (9)
St Nicholas' Chantry CE School, Clevedon

January

First month
Start again, new year
New year's resolutions
Time to diet and lose lots of
Weight.

Ellie Richards (10)
St Nicholas' Chantry CE School, Clevedon

If Only I Had A Pet Dragon

If only I had a pet dragon
I would fly around the world
Go to far places like Spain and Africa.

If only I had a pet dragon
Oh I would have fun
We would go as fast as a motorbike.

If only I had a pet dragon
We would see lots of planes
If we were very lucky we might see a rocket.

If only I had a pet dragon
I could take him to my school
I could even take him on pet day.

If only I had a pet dragon
We could have lots of games
If only I had a pet dragon
I really would have fun.

Chris Warren (7)
St Nicholas' Chantry CE School, Clevedon

Hey Mr Rabbit

Hey Mr Rabbit come out and play
Hey Mr Rabbit it's a lovely day
Come out of your burrow and see the sun.
Hey Mr Rabbit you're number one
Hey Mr Rabbit don't be shy
Hey Mr Rabbit I'll tell you why
I've got loads of carrots for you to eat
Hey Mr Rabbit it's a special treat.

Elle Eisentrager (9)
St Nicholas' Chantry CE School, Clevedon

Midnight

The clock strikes,
Midnight!
Time to come out to play.

The fox creeps,
The badger peeps
Out of its musty den.

The cat prowls
And wise old owl
Hoots in the great oak tree.

The dawn comes
And the sleepy sun
Rises out of bed.

The day has come,
So home we go
We will be back
When midnight strikes.
We will be back
And meet again!

Isabelle Staniaszek (11)
St Nicholas' Chantry CE School, Clevedon

Christmas

C hildren singing in the street
H eavenly angels hear the beat
R inging bells in the street
I t's Christmas time, feel the heat!
S now covers, lush green holly
T is the season to be jolly!
M erry children singing carols
A nd merry adults too!
S o have yourself a merry little
Christmas now!

Sam Smith (9)
St Nicholas' Chantry CE School, Clevedon

The Ocean Whale

The whale is its own
swim teacher.
As it swims swiftly
through the ocean.
It cares for others
around it,
in its own calm and
relaxing way.
Its laid back feature
allows it respect
and space.
So all make way for
the ocean whale!

Annabel Lowe (11)
St Nicholas' Chantry CE School, Clevedon

A Moving Shadow

I saw a moving shadow
last night at twelve.
It scared me like a ghost
and shivered me to my toes.

Then I saw two moving paws,
coming closer, closer and closer.
Some black and white stripes,
and a little shiny nose.

Then I saw another,
tall, thin, dressed in black.
Then I saw a small dark box
and then the shadow was gone!

Molly Frazer-Cann (10)
St Nicholas' Chantry CE School, Clevedon

My Mum

My mum washes my clothes
She cooks my dinner
Irons my clothes.

My mum cleans the house
She looks after me
She helps me if I don't
Understand something.

I love my mum
But best of all
She loves me!

Eloise Maidment (9)
St Nicholas' Chantry CE School, Clevedon

Swimming

Splosh goes the water,
when I dive into the pool.

Splish, goes the water,
when I do front crawl.

Bubbles goes the water,
when I swim down to the bottom.

Splash goes the water,
when I jump up for air.

Slap goes the water,
when I climb out on the side,

Drip goes the water,
when I rush to get dry.

Emily Harden (8)
St Nicholas' Chantry CE School, Clevedon

The Three Wise Men

Wise men from the east
Travel far to seek
The new king born to rule
From Bethlehem so small.

Herod not too pleased
But he fell down on his knees
He had to travel too
To see if it was true.

Wise men from the east
With gifts so they can please
Gold, frankincense and myrrh
Were the gifts they carried in
For baby Jesus the king!

Kelly Youde (11)
St Nicholas' Chantry CE School, Clevedon

The Sea

The candyfloss looking waves
Slipped silently onto the beach.
The sun shone on the crystal clear waves,
As they lashed out at the rocks.
The beach started to wake up slowly.
The wind rose, darting up and the boats started to sail.
The light rippling water sprayed salt at the boats.

The sky got darker and darker,
It started to rain and the waves danced in the storm.
Boats battled with the rough waves to get to the safety
Of the beach.

The rushing waves stopped
And the sky was sparkling and clear.
The raging storm was over,
Fishermen safe at last,
Dancing, diving water.

Suzanne Cunning (10)
St Nicholas' Chantry CE School, Clevedon

The Midnight Cat

I'm going to tell you a story today
About a dream that I once had
It's about a cat, a midnight cat
That made my thoughts go mad!

I was outside with this midnight cat
It was midnight so it was dark
This midnight cat prowled across my garden
Then out across the park.

I followed this mysterious cat
And came upon a tree
I peered through a crack in the trunk
Then guess what I could see!

Some glowing yellow eyes I saw
That unmistakably belonged to bats
But behind these bats there was something else
A swarm of midnight cats!

They must have been this cat's family
As they all looked exactly the same
They were running around and prancing
I think it was some kind of game.

These midnight cats were sleek and slender
With coats of glossy black
Their eyes a piercing crystal green
I just couldn't turn my back.

I looked from the window when I awoke next morn
I squinted from the sun's bright ray
But in the distance, I could plainly see
The midnight cat slinking away.

Becky Heyes (11)
St Nicholas' Chantry CE School, Clevedon

Hope, Fear, Love And Death

Hope: Hope is white, pure and pale,
it smells like the scent of flowers,
it tastes like strawberries and cream
and sounds like a baby bird twittering,
it feels like a pink, silky cushion,
which lives in the heart of my guardian angel.

Fear: Fear is black,
with a smell like rotten apples,
it tastes like red blood,
it sounds like a wolf howling
and feels like a hard, rough rock,
it lives in the heart of a fox.

Love: Love is pink
and smells like roses,
with a taste like creamy white chocolate,
it sounds like a baby laughing,
with a feel like a silky, white blanket,
it lives within the heart of me.

Death: Death is black,
with a smell so stale,
it tastes like blood
and sounds like a hound dog howling,
it feels like water, like red wine dripping
and lives in the heart of the rainforest.

Ashby Vaughan (9)
St Nicholas' Chantry CE School, Clevedon

The Tiger

The tiger tall and sleek
Strides through the forest,
Unrevealed to the naked eye,
Venturing towards its target,
He strikes faster than light
And catches his prey!

Alix Blease (9)
St Nicholas' Chantry CE School, Clevedon

My Family

I'll start with Mum and Dad
The core of my special story
They're full of love and laughter
With strong arms wrapped around me

Dan, my older brother
Is cool, strong and funny
He likes to wind me up
But is a good friend really

I am the star of this family
Although others may not agree
I like to giggle, chat and play
For that is truly me

As you can plainly see
My family is the best
I think it's love that helps us out
That's what I'd suggest!

Katie Lewis (10)
St Nicholas' Chantry CE School, Clevedon

Kenning

Mad barking
Sneaky thief
Hole digging
Bone burying
Fun loving
Cat chasing
Loyal friend
Ball chasing, drooling
Loopy Loo
I love you.

Chellan Noon (10)
St Nicholas' Chantry CE School, Clevedon

Magic Tree

Magic tree,
Your bright greenness,
Catches the eye.

Your balls and lights,
The star above,
Angels of the sky.

Magic tree,
Kept in the loft,
I hear you cry.

Let me discover,
Your magic spell
And let you glisten.

Emma Warren (10)
St Nicholas' Chantry CE School, Clevedon

Once Upon A Rhyme

Once upon a rhyme,
There was a sign
And that sign told the time
And the time was five to nine.

Wow, once upon a time,
Yeah, in the land of rhyme,
Wow, it's a wonderful place,
Yeah and there's loads of space.

Once under the Rhine,
I had a mine,
Filled with jewels that shine
And they were all mine.

Wow, once upon a time,
Yeah, in the land of rhyme,
Wow, it's a wonderful place,
Yeah and there's loads of space!

Lucy Tucker (9)
St Nicholas' Chantry CE School, Clevedon

Morning Hack

Up in the morning at the crack of dawn
Getting dressed in clothes that are warm
The sun is rising up over the hills as I leave
The grass is frosty and I feel a chill.

See the horse's head poking out
As I run I give them a shout
Over I go to feed them hay
They say hello with a snort and a neigh!

I go over and get the tack
To get ready for a hack
Up I jump on his back
Then we trot down the country track.

Off I go cantering away
My horse's tail is trailing behind
It's a beautiful day with adventures
And excitement to find.

All too soon my ride is over
The stable doors are locked
I switch out the lights
And wave to my horse and whisper,
Goodnight.

Harriet Comer (9)
St Nicholas' Chantry CE School, Clevedon

I Like Reading Books

I read small books
I read big books
I read skinny books
I read fat books
I read nonsense books
I read alphabet books
I read poetry books
I read story books
How I like reading books.

Becky Garland (7)
St Nicholas' Chantry CE School, Clevedon

The Sad Owl

High up in a tree,
Was a sour faced owl,
Upon his face,
Was a permanent scowl.

He never did smile
And nobody knew why,
Until one day when he started to cry.

All the animals in the wood,
Gathered round to see,
What was wrong with the owl
High up, in the tree.

I sit on my own, up so very high,
I'm so scared that I can't fly.
I feel lonely, sad, unhappy and mad
And I feel like this every day.
Nobody likes me, nobody cares
And nobody asks me to play.

The animals said, 'We like you, we care,'
And we want you to come and play,
But first of all you must flap your wings
And learn to fly today.

Chloe Vaughan (10)
St Nicholas' Chantry CE School, Clevedon

Guess Who We Are

We are diving gracefully in the water,
Playing playfully.
Our swimming and diving is rapidly flowing.
We ascend from the water fluently and descend gracefully.
We swim to the bottomless oceans.
We are natural, our spirit is wild and free.
We have a silhouette that is beautiful in sunset.
We sing beautifully and make a clickety-clackety sound.
Guessed who we are?

Kathryn Mortimore (9)
St Nicholas' Chantry CE School, Clevedon

The Blackboard

Black, black as night with only stars of chalk to break
the darkness.
Who am I?
Dark, always dark, eternal darkness,
Sunless, mystic darkness.
The only light the flaky chalk.
What am I?

George Carpenter (11)
St Nicholas' Chantry CE School, Clevedon

Before The Match

Supporters,
cheer me,
players,
help me,
coach,
guide me,
football pitch,
create a path
to the goal,
as I go to score
so may
the teammates
all have fun and play well.
As the ball reaches the pitch
so may I
kick it well and far.
Yelling crowd cheer me,
football pitch praise me,
rolling ball, come to me,
lead me to the goal.

Billie-Anne Bethell (8)
Sedgemoor Manor Community Junior School, Somerset

Before I Go To Gymnastics

No injuries,
hurt me,
warm ups,
stretch me,
stretch jumps,
straighten me,
as I jump
off the beam
or do tuck jumps.
The end of the lesson
wears me out.
As I put the
mats away
I do the splits
again.
Balance come
to me,
lead me back home.

Emma Withers (8)
Sedgemoor Manor Community Junior School, Somerset

My Bird

I have a bird called Page
That lives in a round cage,
And eats lots of food
Which is terribly rude.

My bird is rather fat
And gets chased by cats,
So that is my bird,
My bird called Page.

Carla Lambert (11)
Sedgemoor Manor Community Junior School, Somerset

Animals

I think animals are fluffy,

L ovely and cute,
O strich and worm,
V egetarian,
E lephant or mouse.

A nimals are loving,
N o fur or with fur,
I don't really care,
M ad and calm,
A ccurate,
L ovely or ugly,
S ad or happy.

T ongue or eyes,
H air or skin,
E verything,
Y ou, me love . . .

A nimals!
R eally cute,
E specially

C unning or artless
U nder pressure
T iny or huge
E verything I need,
Animals!

Jessie Cresswell (9)
Sedgemoor Manor Community Junior School, Somerset

Before The Football Match

Players,
play me,
goalie,
save me,
teammates,
bless me,
sunny sky,
light my way
through the pitch.
As the ball
goes past the keeper
so may I
be the first
to score a goal.
As the ball
hits the net
so may I
escape the opponent
as he fouls.
Teammates cheer me
goalkeeper save the ball
Teasing opponent
do not injure me,
lead me to the goal.

Michael Hill (9)
Sedgemoor Manor Community Junior School, Somerset

Love

Love is bright, bright red,
It tastes like sweet strawberries,
It smells like freshly baked cakes with cherries on top,
It sounds like beautiful birds singing in the trees,
It looks like lovely flowers flying through the air,
It feels like pillows on a comfy bed.

Macauley Taylor (7)
Sedgemoor Manor Community Junior School, Somerset

Before Bedtime

Mattress
comfort me
quilt
keep me snug
pyjamas
keep me warm.
Bedtime keeps
me cosy and
warm at night
as it darkens
I stay snug
the same way
as any other
person.
When it's midnight
the clock strikes twelve
everyone is asleep.
Barn owls near me
London clock
strikes twelve
quilt
stay with me
lead me to my bed.

Andrew Puk (8)
Sedgemoor Manor Community Junior School, Somerset

Elvis

There was a young man called Elvis
Who had a wiggly pelvis.
He sang all day and night
Until the stars were bright.
He wrote a couple of songs,
He got a bit of a bong.

Dean Marcer (10)
Sedgemoor Manor Community Junior School, Somerset

Before My Dinner

Cooling steam,
surround me,
burning cooker
cook for me,
cold water,
refresh me,
cooking pans,
boil my rice,
puffy and nice.
As the food
reaches my mouth,
slowly I feel something
inside that inspires
my mind with food,
as I take
another bite of
hot, boiling rice as it cooks.
Helpful kitchen cook food
Dirty sink clean my pans
Cooling steam go down please
Take me to my dinner.

Shannon Cooper (9)
Sedgemoor Manor Community Junior School, Somerset

Guinea Pigs

Two little guinea pigs
Both in their beds,
Looking like wigs,
Nodding their heads.
Open the door,
Then take a peek,
Give them an apple core
And listen to them squeak.

Kim Dibble (10)
Sedgemoor Manor Community Junior School, Somerset

Before School

My friends
hear me,
teachers
listen to me,
my friends
help me,
school friends
play with me,
as we play in the playground
so may I leave this school
happy every day.
As the bully stalks his prey
so may I be first to hit the bully
living school hear me,
lead me to this great school.

Ashlea Keirle (9)
Sedgemoor Manor Community Junior School, Somerset

My Lovely Lesson

Miss Triggol,
ask me,
teacher,
help me,
lesson,
praise me,
pencil,
guide me through my lesson
to write a poem to Heaven.
LSA,
help me throughout the glorious day,
ruler,
help me to draw a straight line,
so Miss says it's fine.

Chelsea Dando (9)
Sedgemoor Manor Community Junior School, Somerset

Before The Game

Fast goalie,
hear me.
Cheering fans,
cheer me.
Teammates,
hail me.
Referee
make sure
that the game is fair.
As the goalie protects
the lonely goal
so may I be first to
take a shot.
As the goalie defends the goal
so may I be first to tackle the opponent.
Teams mates, win the game,
opponents lose for me,
lead me to winning.

Ellis Scott (9)
Sedgemoor Manor Community Junior School, Somerset

I Love Animals

I love animals,
Scruffy or not,
Large or tiny,
No matter what.

I love animals,
Big or small,
Ugly or cute,
No difference at all.

I love animals,
Dirty or clean,
Smelly or not,
No difference to me.

Gemma Ransted (10)
Sedgemoor Manor Community Junior School, Somerset

Alphabet Poem

A is for an astonishing, alphabet apple
B is for a blue, bubbling basket
C is for a creepy, crawling cat
D is for delicious, doughy doughnuts
E is for an enormous, elegant elephant
F is for a frightening, freaky frankfurter
G is for great, giant gold
H is for a horrible, haunted house
I is for interesting, inky insects
J is for Jack and the jumping jeans
K is for a kind, kicking koala
L is for lucky little Lucy
M is for mini, monkey mouse
N is for naughty, nasty newts
O is for an octopus opening oysters
P is for porky, pink panthers
Q is for a queer, questioning queen
R is for red, riding rabbit
S is for the silver, silky sun
T is for tiny, twinkling tortoise
U is for a unicorn under an umbrella
V is for a vertical, violent vulture
W is for the wicked witch of the west
X is for xylophone, X-raying and Xmas
Y is for yellow, yucky yeast
Z is for a zippy zebra zipping.

Kyomi Chilcott (9)
Sedgemoor Manor Community Junior School, Somerset

Circle

Oh, why am I a circle?
I want to be a snail,
But now I've changed my mind,
I'd rather be a whale.

Antonia Wilmot (8)
Sedgemoor Manor Community Junior School, Somerset

Alphabet Poem

A is for Annie, Annie apple
B is for Benjamin, Benjamin bunny
C is for cat, cautious cat
D is for dog, dotty dog
E is for elephant, enormous elephant
F is for Fred, fireman Fred
G is for green, graffiti green
H is for hairy, hairy hat man
I is for ink, inky ink
J is for Josie, Josie jump
K is for king, kicking king
L is for Lucy, Lucy lamp lady
M is for Mike, munching Mike
N is for Nick, naughty Nick
O is for octopus, orange octopus
P is for picture, pinky picture
Q is for queen, quacking queen
R is for Ritchie, Ritchie robber
S is for Sammy, Sammy snake
T is for teapot, titchy teapot
U is for umbrella, ugly umbrella
V is for Viking, vicious Viking
W is for witch, wicked witch
X is for xylophone, X-raying xylophone
Y is for yacht, yellow yacht
Z is for zebra, zippy zebra.

Lewis Baker (10)
Sedgemoor Manor Community Junior School, Somerset

Pets

Cats miaow and are scared of hoses,
Dogs bark and twitch their noses.
Birds tweet and sing a song,
While fish blow bubbles all day long.

Ashlee Rawles (10)
Sedgemoor Manor Community Junior School, Somerset

I Love Sweets

I love sweets

L ounging round and scoffing them
O h how lovely candyfloss melts in your mouth
V iolet drops make me go hyper
E ating red cherries from the south.

S weets are just lovely
W hen I get chocolate cake
E xcept when I go to the dentist, he says
E ating it will make my teeth ache
T esting on my jaws I think . . .
S weets are not gorgeous anymore.

Sophie Cole (9)
Sedgemoor Manor Community Junior School, Somerset

Ghost

Last night I heard a funny noise,
When I got into bed.
I thought I was imagining it,
I thought it was all in my head.

I walked across the landing,
Holding my candle with care.
Was there something at the other side?
I stop, I stand, I stare.

I start to walk,
The floorboards creak,
It frightens me to death,
Then I see somebody peek,
It takes away my breath!

Emma Baker (10)
Sedgemoor Manor Community Junior School, Somerset

Fireworks

F rying in the night sky
I ntruding on the dazzling stars
R ough colours spraying in the wind
E xploding with a bang
W hizzing up in the sky
O range and emerald
R ockets opening like a flower
K eeping the stars hidden
S hining in the night sky.

Chloé Bowen (10)
Sedgemoor Manor Community Junior School, Somerset

Here Lies The Body

Here lies the body of
William Weep,
Run down by a car
That could not beep.

Here lies the body of
Beefy Bert,
Bit by a dog,
That must hurt.

Here lies the body of
Horsy Hannah,
Hit down by a very
Huge banner.

Here lies the body of
Abandoned Ann,
She got hardly any food
But could do the can-can.

And there I end my
List of the dead,
Because I was just hit
By a rock on the head.

Stephanie Lee (9)
Sedgemoor Manor Community Junior School, Somerset

My Dog

My dog is great,
He rolls around in the mud
And digs up the grass.
He blows bubbles in the water.

He drinks from the pond
And chases the cats.
He goes for a walk
But I have to clean up!

Connor Keirle (10)
Sedgemoor Manor Community Junior School, Somerset

Snow

Never seen the snow so white,
Which comes once a year,
Through the glistening rain,
From the skies above.

I stood outside
In the falling snow,
It came so hard
That it blew me away.

I went back inside,
To tell my mum
That the snow blew me away
From the end of the street to the start.

My mum said, 'No,
You must be joking.'
I said, 'Come out,'
And she finally believed me.

Lauren Huxtable (10)
Sedgemoor Manor Community Junior School, Somerset

Caring For Your Teeth

Clean your teeth twice a day,
If you don't they will decay.

Keep your teeth in good care,
If you don't they won't be there!

Please listen,
Otherwise you're riskin',
Your precious teeth.

Heidi Creech (10)
Sedgemoor Manor Community Junior School, Somerset

Before The Match

Players,
help me,
jumpy goalie,
save goals,
supporters,
cheer me on,
soft grass,
lead me
to the goal.
As the opponents
try to tackle me
let me score a goal
on this football pitch.
As the other team gets the ball
let me tackle and get it back.
Players get goals,
soft ground let me run,
teammates let me have a chance,
lead me to win.

Stephanie Cox (9)
Sedgemoor Manor Community Junior School, Somerset

Winter

In the winter
I wear jumpers,
Gloves, a scarf.
When I go out
It is snowy,
Freezing cold.
When I go to bed
I take a hot water bottle.
When I walk out in the cold
I get pink cheeks.
It is really slippery on the road and path.
I have to wear a coat.
It is really windy.
I get snow-blown.
I catch a cold.

Alannah Saunders (10)
Sedgemoor Manor Community Junior School, Somerset

Winter

Frosty ground and it's cold,
The grass is damp,
The sun gleams and beams,
The night is cold and frosty,
You need to wrap up
In ear muffs,
A hat,
A coat,
A scarf.
The sun slips,
Dips into night
Like a closing mouth,
An icy floor, frosty cars,
Damp trees,
It's winter.

Kathleen Upton (10)
Sedgemoor Manor Community Junior School, Somerset

Before The Tennis Match

Teammates,
Whack it.
Supporters,
Cheer me.
Everyone
Help us,
Get into position
To pass the ball!
Jump up very high
And pull the racquet back,
Then whack it forward.
As it darkens
We pack away.
On the way home I see a flying racquet.
When I get in the door I hear a noise,
It's a flying tennis racquet!
Lead me to my room.

Ellie Davis (8)
Sedgemoor Manor Community Junior School, Somerset

My Pets

Pets are quite loving things,
They like to lie on comfy things.

I have a dog
That chases frogs.
I have a fish
That lives in a round dish.
I have a cat
That loves to eat rats.

My dog's called Ross,
He acts like a boss.
My fish is called Pip,
He likes to nip.
My cat's called Molly,
She has a squeaky dolly.

Abby Mitchell (10)
Sedgemoor Manor Community Junior School, Somerset

The Four Seasons

Spring days are cosy and warm,
The sheep have lambs that are newborn.

Summer days are hot and sunny,
Bees come out and make their honey.

Autumn days are chilly and bitter,
The leaves fall down and look like litter.

Winter days are cold and jolly,
Berries come out and join the holly.

These four seasons put together
Make up the whole year's weather.

If one of these seasons was not to be,
It would be like a lock without a key.

Jasmine Lewis (11)
Sedgemoor Manor Community Junior School, Somerset

It's Wintertime

The weather in winter is full of chilly mice
Who slide on ice.
When they eat cheese all the fleas start moving about.

I see the snow is blowing in the air,
While a big bear is roaring and snoring,
The smell of ice stinks of mice.

I wear a waterproof jacket
And carry a packet of crisps.

I go on the slides over at the fair
Where all the riders are.

There was a snowman full of rubbish cans.

Ian Dando (10)
Sedgemoor Manor Community Junior School, Somerset

The Football Match

Teammates
Help me.
Players pass
To me.
Manager don't
Hit me.
Football pitch
Make me win.
As the goalie
Protects the
Moving ball,
So may only just
Win this really
Fantastic game.
As my friends
Cheer for me.
So Lord please make
Me and my team win.
Howling trees hear me,
Cold wind stop my heart.
Manager if we lose please
Take it out on me.

Rebecca Broome (8)
Sedgemoor Manor Community Junior School, Somerset

My Dog Stanley

Stanley is the most loveable dog,
He's old and grey
And loves custard creams.
He is the littlest Yorkie you could meet,
Who loves warmth and heat
And lives in the land of dreams.

T-Anna Buxton (11)
Sedgemoor Manor Community Junior School, Somerset

Animals Are Cute

A ny animal is cute
N ot one of them isn't
I f big or small
M akes no difference
A ny animal is cute no matter what
L ight or dark
S o don't take the lot.

A ny animal is cute no matter what
R at or mouse
E lephant or deer.

C ute as can be
U gly doesn't come in
T ough or weak
E ating animals isn't right so lock everybody up with a key.

Shannon Adams (10)
Sedgemoor Manor Community Junior School, Somerset

The Wondrous Lake

One dusky nigh
As the sun sank slowly on the horizon,
The beautiful swans cast a reflection
On the shining lake.
Is that an elephant I see?

The pink wispy clouds floated
Like a flamingo in the sky,
An outline of a distant moon glimmered
Like a white veil.
As I glanced up at the jagged red rocks,
A scrawny man marvelled at this astonishing place.

Holly Miller (10)
Sedgemoor Manor Community Junior School, Somerset

The Haunted Mansion

Howling of ghouls,
Clanging of bells.
Scratching of claws,
A decaying smell!

The stairs haunted by a nameless person,
Suits of armour gleaming in the moonlight.
The deserted mansion
With a darkening sight.

Howling of ghouls,
Clanging of bells.
Scratching of claws,
What a decaying smell!

Tables that creak,
A ghost maiden creeps.
In the garden they reap,
Their breath really reeks.

Howling of ghouls,
Clanging of bells.
Scratching of claws,
A decaying smell!

Adam Busby (11)
Sedgemoor Manor Community Junior School, Somerset

Milkshakes

I like milkshakes a whole lot,
Plenty of it that's what I've got,
Drinking it from a straw it's so creamy,
Um! It's really dreamy,
Oh yeah that's my style,
I'll drink vanilla for a while,
But I prefer chocolate, I can't even wait.
Whatever is your favourite, I'll bet it's great.

Keeley Jones (11)
Sedgemoor Manor Community Junior School, Somerset

School Trip

Last week my class went on a mountain hike,
We had to stay the night.
The teacher brought a book to read,
Jenny brought some food to control her greed.
Becky brought her group of bears,
Sam brought her Barbie fair.

Midnight came
And we played our game
While the teacher fell asleep,
With his book on his feet.
Then we heard a loud sound
And hid under the sleeping bags,
But it turned out to be
The janitor making a cup of tea.

Heather Cooke (11)
Sedgemoor Manor Community Junior School, Somerset

Notes

I was here, not for long,
Left my name to turn you on.
If it works you are class,
If it didn't eat some glass.
Run to the toilet with a dog,
Come out with a hog,
Give it a big snog.
Put it to the floor,
Ram it out the door.
Buy a light,
Attach it to a kite,
Tie a note, write on it,
'I'm sending again a note
What only I wrote,
Don't send one again.'
Or I'll be back again.

Thomas Baker (10)
Sedgemoor Manor Community Junior School, Somerset

Before The Match

Teammates
Hear me.
Goalie
Defend the goal.
Opposition
Don't injure me.
Teammates create a path
To the opposition goal.
As the defenders and goalie
Defend the lonely goal,
So I may
Escape the injury
On this football pitch.
As the strikers
Shoot at the goal
So may the
Goalkeeper defend the goal.
Teammates hear me,
Teammates let us win
And the opposition lose!
Let us win the match.

Ben Pearce (9)
Sedgemoor Manor Community Junior School, Somerset

Football

I like to play football,
I like to run around,
I'd like to watch Liverpool
And be a member of the crowd!

I'd like to meet Owen
And shake his hand,
Definitely knowing
He's the best footballer in the land!

Harriet Bethell (11)
Sedgemoor Manor Community Junior School, Somerset

Before The Match

Teammates
Listen up,
Supporters
Cheer me,
David Bekcham
Help me,
Football pitch
Make a passage
To the goal.
As the goalie protects
The lonely goal
So may I
Escape the opponent
On the football pitch.
As the opponent
Makes a plan
So may I
Be first to score a goal.
Teammates do my plan,
That will make it easy,
Opponents let me win,
Lead me to the ball.

Joshua Jones (9)
Sedgemoor Manor Community Junior School, Somerset

Dolphins

D iving
O bscure
L ovely
P layful
H ilarious
I ntelligent
N ice
S wimmer.

Hayley Moule (10)
Sedgemoor Manor Community Junior School, Somerset

Before The Tables Test

Concentration
Stay with me,
Writing to be
Quick for me,
Nerves
Stick with me,
Teachers
Go slow with me to the end.
As the numbers
On the lonely page
So may I
Make them right
For the teacher Mr Thomas.
As teacher Mr Thomas
Takes the score
So may I
Be first to get a high score.
Teachers please congratulate me,
Friends be there for me.
Teacher, teacher smile at me,
Lead me to a high score.

Dannielle Gillard (9)
Sedgemoor Manor Community Junior School, Somerset

My Poem

A car stopped at my gate today,
But the only problem was he's too late!
So I shouted, 'Go away you're too late.'
The next day I stood in some clay
When the door knocked so I went to answer it,
No one was there, I shouted madly, 'Who is it?'
Soon he sat down on the mat
And then he sat down on the cat.

Matty Hall (7)
Sedgemoor Manor Community Junior School, Somerset

Before I Go To Osmington Bay

Clever teachers
Hear me,
Coach drivers
Hail me,
Mum and Dad
Calm me,
Guiding friends
Light my
Way through the wait.
As the coach
Drives away
So may I
Say goodbye to all my
Friends and family.
As the people
Watch and cry
So may they
Say a big goodbye.
People whimpering hear me,
Mum and Dad steal my heart,
Coach driver smile with me,
Osmington Bay here we come.

Rebecca Gooding (9)
Sedgemoor Manor Community Junior School, Somerset

Limos

Limos are long,
Limos are stretchy,
Limos blow smoke
And it goes on forever
And it won't stop.
Limos are long,
Limos are cool.

Jordan Lee (7)
Sedgemoor Manor Community Junior School, Somerset

Before The Times Table Test

Concentration
Help me.
Teachers
Teach me.
Homework
Stick with me.
Teachers slow down
With me.
As I wait
For the next sum,
Make me write
In this table test.
Teachers please clap
For me,
So may I
Be first to get the sums.
Large brain, keep concentration,
Cheating go away from me,
Lead me to my score.

Gemma Lambert (8)
Sedgemoor Manor Community Junior School, Somerset

Love

Love looks like deep red,
It smells like the smell of summer,
It tastes like lots of chocolate,
It sounds like discos going on,
It feels like you're snuggled up in bed.

Sarah Howe (8)
Sedgemoor Manor Community Junior School, Somerset

The House

In the house all I could hear was the squeak of a mouse
Or was it a mouse?
I walked up the stairs and all of my hair stood three inches high.
From nowhere the shrill cry of a lonely girl.
I broke the door down and saw what I saw.

The howling of the wolf,
The cry of the ghouls,
The scratching of an innocent claw.

On the roof I looked and there it was,
An object decaying under the midnight bloom,
I glanced upwards,
She was as green as a rotting bean,
I saw what I saw.

The howling of the wolf,
The cry of the ghouls,
The scratching of an innocent claw.

In the garden she stood next to the rotting growth,
Her head swaying vigorously like a cold winter's gale,
I saw what I saw.

The howling of the wolf,
The cry of the ghouls,
The scratching of an innocent claw.

Joshua Godfrey (11)
Sedgemoor Manor Community Junior School, Somerset

Happiness

Happiness is a bright, shining yellow,
It tastes like a lovely yellow sweet,
It smells like a yellow banana ripening in the fruit bowl,
It sounds like a hot yellow, bright sun sizzling in the sky,
It looks like a bright yellow light flashing in the street,
It feels like the soft sand on a beach.

Lauren Whiteley (8)
Sedgemoor Manor Community Junior School, Somerset

Winter

The weather is cold and frosty,
It's snow all around,
Blue sky,
White clouds,
Mist in the air,
Fresh cold breath.
You see snow
Around the ground.
Trees naked,
Leaves on the floor,
Ponds frozen.
Gloves to keep your hands warm,
Coats to keep your body dry.
A sweater to keep your chest
And stomach warm.
In winter you can
Snowboard downhill,
Riding on a sleigh,
Snowball fight with friends,
Ice skating on icy ponds.

Max Matthews (11)
Sedgemoor Manor Community Junior School, Somerset

Money

M ountains of money shining in the sun,
O h, what can we spend it on? Lots of fun,
N ice toys and treats,
E ven sweets, for
Y ou and me.

Chloe Creech (8)
Sedgemoor Manor Community Junior School, Somerset

Before Maths Test

Mr Thomas
Hear me,
Times tables
Come to me,
My friends
Help me,
Zooming teacher
Light my way
Through the test.
As the children
Protect their maths books,
So may I
Escape the tables
In this crowded room.
As the teacher
Stalks the class
So may I
Be first to spy my page.
Living room help me,
Still wind slow my heart,
Teasing shadows write with me,
Lead me to my test.

Georgia Saunders (8)
Sedgemoor Manor Community Junior School, Somerset

Anger

Anger is a dark, dark blue,
It tastes like lemon pineapple pie,
Sugar spread over the top.
It smells like a strawberry fresh smell all over.
It sounds like people fighting all over the place.
It looks like dark dreams flying over the moon.
It feels like rough sandpaper.

Charmaine Thorne (8)
Sedgemoor Manor Community Junior School, Somerset

Before The Match

Teammates
Help me,
Supporting fans
Like me,
Opponents tackle me,
Golden ball guide my
Way down the pitch.
As the defenders guard the try line
So may I score a goal on this rugby pitch.
As the ball goes over the line
So may I score a goal,
Living pitch let me score,
Teammates pass to me so I can score a goal
To lead us to victory.

Samuel Pear (9)
Sedgemoor Manor Community Junior School, Somerset

In The Winter

In the winter it's cool, it's cold,
Frosty white air is crisp,
Ground is crunchy,
People skating, slipping, sliding, slipping,
Building snowmen,
Wearing hats.
The sky is coming down with snow,
Can't see where we are going,
Snow is blocking the way.
Snow is coming down hard,
I can't sleep in the silence.

Anthony Collins (11)
Sedgemoor Manor Community Junior School, Somerset

Winter

Snow falls softly on the grass.
The rain is heavy as everybody
Rushes for their waterproofs.
The frost is slippery
And the water turns to ice.
In the winter you light your fires.
In the winter you see people put
Up decoration inside and outside.
Carnival floats go brightly past
People's homes in the winter.
Ice skaters skate on the frozen ponds.

Ben Mills (11)
Sedgemoor Manor Community Junior School, Somerset

Winter Poem

In the cold winter when the snow falls
The hedgehogs curl like a ball,
The sun goes away
But the moon is here to stay.

The rain comes down
And falls around.
The white grass
Is hard to pass.

Thick woolly jumpers,
Thick heavy trousers,
Thick woolly scarves
Keeping me warm. The cold is out.

Making snowball fights,
Making all the amazing sights.
Making bushes white,
Making snowballs in the night.

Sophie Gillard (10)
Sedgemoor Manor Community Junior School, Somerset

Seasons

A little spring shower,
A very sunny day,
A gush of wind with force and power
And snow on a winter's day.

In the spring lambs are born,
In the summer you bathe all day.
In autumn farmers harvest the corn
And in the winter you want to play.

Stephanie Nichols (11)
Sedgemoor Manor Community Junior School, Somerset

Seasons

Winter, summer, autumn, spring,
In the winter I hear bells ring.
Summertime is really hot.
In spring I have a flower pot.
When autumn comes the leaves go crunch.
All year round flowers in a bunch.

Emily Ives (10)
Sedgemoor Manor Community Junior School, Somerset

Love

Love is deep red,
It tastes like a new apple,
It smells like a sugared lemon,
It sounds like birds singing in the trees,
It looks like a smiling sun,
It feels like the soft snow.

Emily Lowe (7)
Sedgemoor Manor Community Junior School, Somerset

Months Of The Year

January, cold but fun,
Catching snowflakes on your tongue.

February brings rain again,
Rain running down your windowpane.

Springtime March brings out the sun,
Lots of children having fun.

April leaves growing on the trees,
See the little bumblebees.

In May new animals being born,
The sky is blue, it's getting warm.

June sun flashes on the flowers,
After school children play out for hours.

July sun brings boiling days,
So everyone goes out to play.

August brings out red-hot sun,
It sees the children having fun.

September brings the colder nights,
Windows full of candlelight.

Cold October brings a breeze,
It makes our toes and fingers freeze.

November, the eleventh month of the year,
Sometimes it's cloudy, sometimes clear.

December brings frosty white,
Although it's dark, each night is bright.

3PS Literacy Class
Sedgemoor Manor Community Junior School, Somerset

Before The World Cup

Football friends
hear me,
dancing keepers
praise me.
Teammates
guide me,
through the
World Cup.
Let me
win the
game.
Guide my
way through
the pitch.
As the ball
goes past
the keeper
so may I
be first
to cheer.
As the crowd
starts cheering
when we score
the last remaining
goal we'll be
able to hold the
World Cup.

Zak Mountford (8)
Sedgemoor Manor Community Junior School, Somerset

Love

Love is deep red,
It tastes like a juicy and sour orange,
It smells like fresh cream on a chocolate cake,
It sounds like loud music in the carnival,
It looks like a garden full of stones,
It feels like a squashy, cuddly teddy.

Harry Winchester (7)
Sedgemoor Manor Community Junior School, Somerset

Happiness

Happiness looks like a bright blue.
Happiness tastes like a great orange, juicy and sweet.
Happiness sounds like a hummingbird.
Happiness feels like a soft pillow.
Happiness smells like a fresh flower.
Happiness is a beautiful pink.

Stephan-Lüc Chandler (7)
Sedgemoor Manor Community Junior School, Somerset

Hedgehogs

Spiky,
Prickly, round
And small,
All screwed up as
Round as a ball.
Prickles are hard,
Spiky and sharp.
Hedgehogs only
Come out in the dark.

Lauren Whitehouse (8)
Sedgemoor Manor Community Junior School, Somerset

Winter

White winter weather,
Cold as a freezer,
Snow blowing,
Icy cold crisp air.

Snowmen dancing in the icy wind,
Frosty lakes and frosty ponds,
Robins in the sky fly so high,
Bare branches icing up.

Nice warm chocolate
To fill me up
And make me warm
When I'm in bed.

Play in the snow,
Making snowmen,
Calling on my friends,
Play with snowballs.

Things looking different,
Everything white.
Houses have snow on the roofs
And the grass is white.

Amber Milne (10)
Sedgemoor Manor Community Junior School, Somerset

Father Christmas

Father Christmas is funny,
he carries the toys on his tummy.
He comes down the chimney,
puts the presents on the floor
and runs to the next door.

Bethany Addicott (8)
Sedgemoor Manor Community Junior School, Somerset

Listen

Listen!
What can you hear?
The crashing rain
And my mum being a pain.

Listen!
What can you hear?
The crashing thunder
And the light of the lightning,
Oh it's frightening.

Listen!
What can you hear?
Children playing and having fun
When they are out in the sun.

Alice Day (8)
Sedgemoor Manor Community Junior School, Somerset

Inside My Head

Inside my head I am blue,
Inside my head I have the flu.
Inside my head I am thinking of you,
Inside my head it's true.
Inside my head I have a son,
Inside my head I'm having fun.
Inside my head it's red,
Inside my head it's dead.
Inside my head I am a cat,
Inside my head I am a rat.
Inside my head I am in my car,
Inside my head I am going far.

Carla Selway (8)
Sedgemoor Manor Community Junior School, Somerset

Sadness

Sadness is a deep dark blue,
It smells like the seaside.
It tastes like butter,
Strong and horrible lemon.
It looks like an angel floating in the light blue sky.
It feels like the sun burning my feet.

Zoe Winter (7)
Sedgemoor Manor Community Junior School, Somerset

Love

Love is a deep red,
It smells like sweet perfume.
And tastes like juicy strawberries.
Love shines in the air
And sounds like birds twittering in the trees.
It feels like a comfy pillow.

Rosa Mantle (8)
Sedgemoor Manor Community Junior School, Somerset

My Baby Brother

My baby brother is really good,
Every night he gets out of his bed
He is still being good to me.
I don't mind if he is naughty,
My baby brother is ever so sweet
Even when he sucks his feet.
He loves the bath a lot,
I love him so much!

Natasha Cross (7)
Sedgemoor Manor Community Junior School, Somerset

How People Live

A is for lovely fresh air,
B is for loving new birth,
C is for proper care,
D is for long old death,
E is for lots of energy,
F is for long, hard, fight,
G is for God, the man who cares,
H is for heart, that should never stop beating,
I is for illness, that should never come,
J is for jog, you need to do,
K is for king, always rich,
L is for love, that's always there,
M is for mother, you should care,
N is for night, that always comes,
O is for organ, take care,
P is for pink, you should always have,
Q is for quiet, save your breath,
R is for read, always good,
S is for shave, stops hairs,
T is for trouble, never get into,
U is for United, always watch,
V is for veins, never break,
W is for water, always drink,
X is for X-ray, always have,
Y is for young, make the most of what you have,
Z is for zombie, goodbye.

Jason Lovegrove (10)
Sedgemoor Manor Community Junior School, Somerset

Roxy

Nose wet as a puddle,
Fur brown as a tree trunk,
Claws sharp as a carving knife,
Tail a puffy carpet,
Very thin skin and soft belly.

Lauren Milverton (8)
Woolavington Primary School, Somerset

Basil

Wet, gooey, squishy nose,
Long, bendy, stretchy tail,
Super shark like claws,
Hard straight paws,
Quick extreme legs,
Giant gaping mouth,
Dotty, spotty tongue,
Destroying, scary tail,
Chases cats like mad,
Runs around,
Gets happy,
Follows people,
Eats quickly,
Goes crazy,
Really, really adores walks.

Liam Perry (7)
Woolavington Primary School, Somerset

The Little White Horse

The little white horse stands in the moonlight,
Raising his horn in great delight,
His beautiful white body so narrow and slender,
His nerves so big and greatly tender,
His head so big and enormously strong,
His mane and tail so silver and long,
His big black eyes so disturbed and tense,
Like something drawing near, something immense.
He gallops on down a great big hill,
He is built with speed and intelligent skill,
The little white horse was never heard of again,
That night when he was disturbed by some horrible men.

Kate Sparrow (9)
Woolavington Primary School, Somerset

Tarantula

Pitch-black legs,
Claws like razors,
Slender black eyes,
Black pygmies, short hair,
Triangular smooth nose,
Circular smooth body,
Head like a rubber.

Nicholas Newton-Mason (7)
Woolavington Primary School, Somerset

School Days Are Fun

S chool days are fun,
C hildren working very well,
H aving lunch and sometimes they eat buns,
O ut goes the school bell,
O utside the children play on the playground,
L earning is fun and everything else is fun.

James Gillett (9)
Woolavington Primary School, Somerset

Hindu Poem

Hindu people pray each night,
To make sure they have a fright,
They dance in the moonlight,
Their looks very, very polite.

They give sweets which they like to bite,
The light makes a beautiful sight.
The gods have a lot of might,
Which brings them good luck for that night.

Farran Stewart (9)
Woolavington Primary School, Somerset

A Cat Called Bunny

A cat called Bunny
He's lovely and funny,
Into my tea he dips
And he licks my lips.
He likes to climb a tree
And licks out of my tea.
He sleeps on my bed
And in the morning he licks my head.
I like bunny,
No wonder why, he's lovely and funny.

Megan Dear (9)
Woolavington Primary School, Somerset

Spring

S hows signs of new life,
P retty pink roses dance in the sunshine,
R ain hardly ever comes,
I n spring it is sunny,
N oisy birds sing at dawn,
G reen grass shimmers brightly.

Iona Neilson (10)
Woolavington Primary School, Somerset

Siva

A pale brown and snow-white colour,
Medium size pointy white ears,
Brown, light, small soft tail,
Legs brown with some creamy white,
Rose-pink tongue.

Victoria Bostock (8)
Woolavington Primary School, Somerset

Henry VIII

Henry VIII had six wives,
But he wrecked all their lives.
He wanted to marry Anne Boleyn,
But she wasn't good enough for him.

Jane Seymour gave him a son,
He was the only one.
In the end Jane died,
Henry VIII cried and cried.

Catherine Parr
Didn't get very far,
Because in the end she died.
Henry VIII said to his mate,
She was the last lady he was going to date.

Rhiannon Larmont (9)
Woolavington Primary School, Somerset

Funny Skeletons

One dark night
Without a fright,
Up they got
Because it was hot.

They raced on bikes
All night,
Without no brakes,
They were a fake.

On their way back,
Forgetting to pack,
Got back in the house
And went to sleep in the 'bone mouse'.

Shane Coombes (9)
Woolavington Primary School, Somerset

Our Pinboard

We're such a busy family
We have to keep a list
Pinned on the kitchen notice board
To make sure nothing's missed.

On Mondays Jack's got swimming,
On Tuesdays I've got dance,
Then later I've got keyboard
And Mel's got flute (advanced).

Wednesdays Mel and I stay on
To practise the school play
While Mum takes Jack to judo
With his best friend, Timmy Ray.

On Thursdays there's just Guides and Cubs
And Fridays are quite slack,
But this week there's Ray's party,
(Ten miles there and back).

Saturdays it's gym and skating,
Football club for Jack.
What a squash with all Mum's shopping
Crammed into the back!

On Sundays Mum takes Mel to choir
And drops me off for riding,
And makes sure Dad's got dinner on
And isn't busy skiving.

But this week we're in trouble -
Mum's nowhere to be seen.
Her note said, 'Relaxation course',
I think that's really mean.

Sophie Connelly (9)
Woolavington Primary School, Somerset

Sweets

S ugary sweets
W hat a treat,
E at, eat, eat,
E xactly
T o me
S aid he.

C aroline
H ates
O range sweets
C os
O nly
L aura
A te
T he
E xotic sweets.

C aroline
R egrets
E ating
A ny
M ars Bars.

Polly-Rose Newcomb (9)
Woolavington Primary School, Somerset

Ruby

Long floppy ears looking like they're sad,
Sky blue eyes matching me!
Tiny, cute, coal black nose,
Smiling mouth like it's always been.
Chequered, brushed furry body,
Effective paws as hard as a rock,
She howls when she's hungry
And jump up. Argh!
I love my dog.

Michael Goodwin (8)
Woolavington Primary School, Somerset

Posh Spice

Posh Spice
Is very nice.
She dances and sings
When she gets the chance.

When David Beckham scores a goal,
She goes, 'Wow! Oh.'

George Dicks (9)
Woolavington Primary School, Somerset

Sweets

Sweets rot your teeth,
They're very good treats.
Chocolate frogs,
Dairy Milk mugs.

Candy canes are sticky,
Humbugs are all licky,
That's what I like.

Chad Cox (9)
Woolavington Primary School, Somerset

Harry

Pointy, spiky sharp claws,
Lengthy sharp teeth,
Tiny, small soft paws,
Long prickly whiskers,
Smooth, tickley tiny legs,
Light white pink nose,
Squidgy body,
Bumpy tongue,
Pointy, furry smooth ears,
Dark blue sunny eyes.

Reece Pople (8)
Woolavington Primary School, Somerset

Poppy

Beaming blue eyes,
Huge hitting paws,
Razor sharp, snapping claws,
Whipping, wagging tail,
Curly, fluffy feet,
Reflective white teeth,
Oval, dark nose,
Loves to lie on mat or bed all day.

Kieran Boobyer (8)
Woolavington Primary School, Somerset

Lita

Pointed brown smooth ears,
Dark brown eyes,
Large wide mouth,
Curled white and brown puffy tail,
Plain white and black legs,
Jet black, damp nose,
Plain snowy foot,
Light pink tongue,
Greasy hard fur,
White transparent whiskers.

Allysha Walford (8)
Woolavington Primary School, Somerset

Dilly Dollops

Long tail like a log,
White as snow,
Black as ebony,
As reflective as the sun,
Rose-pink circular bottom,
Slender shank body,
Likes to eat green biscuits.

Jennifer Bird-Davis (8)
Woolavington Primary School, Somerset

Schooldays

Sitting on your chair, listening to the teacher.
Chatting to your friends, the subject is boring,
Hoping to get out of class,
Out to lunch,
Out to break,
Let's eat, let's play.

Down the steps to class,
Apples and bananas, let's begin the food fight,
Yippee, yippee, time to go home,
Sleep, sleep, is all we need.

Grace Sutton (8)
Woolavington Primary School, Somerset

Kittens And Puppies

Kittens run around,
Kittens play and pound,
Kittens are my best friends,
Kittens all around.

Puppies, puppies everywhere,
Puppies, puppies under the chair,
Puppies, puppies chewing my hair,
Puppies, puppies everywhere.

Evangeline Louisiana Mayor (8)
Woolavington Primary School, Somerset

My Cats

I have two cats at home,
They're even more special than the City of London key,
Not even to swap for Bailey the dog, with our next door neighbour Lee.

I have two cats at home,
They're as sweet as can be,
Misty is all grey and Roxie is white on her tummy and she is tickley.

Roxie will lick your fish with chips
And Misty nicks the sandwich ham and grabs it with her lips.

I love my cats they're always mine,
I'll never let them go,
Not even to trade for a lump of squidgy dough,
They're mine, ho, ho.

Jade Blake (8)
Woolavington Primary School, Somerset

Cats, Dogs, Puppies And Kittens

Puppies and kittens

Puppies and kittens are cute,
Puppies and kittens are sweet,
Puppies and kittens can't live without something to eat

Cats and Dogs

Cats and dogs go out for walks,
Cats and dogs try to talk,
Cats and dogs jump through hoops
And all of their hairs get into loops.

Bethany Etherington (9)
Woolavington Primary School, Somerset